Education Policy

Series Editors

Lance Fusarelli, North Carolina State University
Frederick M. Hess, American Enterprise Institute
Martin West, Harvard University

This series addresses a variety of topics in the area of education policy. Volumes are solicited primarily from social scientists with expertise in education, in addition to policy makers or practitioners with hands-on experience in the field. Topics of particular focus include state and national policy; teacher recruitment, retention, and compensation; urban school reform; test-based accountability; choice-based reform; school finance; higher education costs and access; the quality of instruction in higher education; leadership and administration in K-12 and higher education; teacher colleges; the role of the courts in education policy–making; and the relationship between education research and practice. The series serves as a venue for presenting stimulating new research findings, serious contributions to ongoing policy debates, and accessible volumes that illuminate important questions or synthesize existing research.

Series Editors

LANCE FUSARELLI is professor and director of Graduate Programs in the Department of Leadership, Policy, and Adult and Higher Education at North Carolina State University. He is the coauthor of *Better Policies, Better Schools* and coeditor of the *Handbook of Education Politics and Policy*.

FREDERICK M. HESS is resident scholar and director of Education Policy Studies at the American Enterprise Institute. An author, teacher, and political scientist, his books include *The Same Thing Over and Over: How School Reformers Get Stuck in Yesterday's Ideas* and *Common Sense School Reform*.

MARTIN WEST is assistant professor of Education in the Graduate School of Education at Harvard University. He is an executive editor of *Education Next* and deputy director of Harvard's Program on Education Policy and Governance.

Ohio's Education Reform Challenges: Lessons from the Frontlines
  Chester E. Finn, Jr., Terry Ryan, and Michael B. Lafferty

Accountability in American Higher Education
  Edited by Kevin Carey and Mark Schneider

Freedom and School Choice in American Education
  Edited by Greg Forster and C. Bradley Thompson

Gentrification and Schools: The Process of Integration When Whites Reverse Flight
  Jennifer Burns Stillman

Intersections of Children's Health, Education, and Welfare
  Bruce S. Cooper and Janet D. Mulvey

President Obama and Education Reform: The Personal and the Political
    Robert Maranto and Michael Q. McShane

Educational Policy in an International Context: Political Culture and Its Effects
    Edited by Karen Seashore Louis and Boudewijn van Velzen

The Politics of Parent Choice in Public Education: The Choice Movement in North Carolina and the United States
    Wayne D. Lewis

The Politics of Parent Choice in Public Education

The Choice Movement in North Carolina and the United States

Wayne D. Lewis

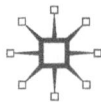

THE POLITICS OF PARENT CHOICE IN PUBLIC EDUCATION
Copyright © Wayne D. Lewis, 2013.

Softcover reprint of the hardcover 1st edition 2013 978-1-137-31207-5
All rights reserved.

First published in 2013 by
PALGRAVE MACMILLAN®
in the United States—a division of St. Martin's Press LLC,
175 Fifth Avenue, New York, NY 10010.

Where this book is distributed in the UK, Europe and the rest of the world, this is by Palgrave Macmillan, a division of Macmillan Publishers Limited, registered in England, company number 785998, of Houndmills, Basingstoke, Hampshire RG21 6XS.

Palgrave Macmillan is the global academic imprint of the above companies and has companies and representatives throughout the world.

Palgrave® and Macmillan® are registered trademarks in the United States, the United Kingdom, Europe and other countries.

ISBN 978-1-349-45714-4   ISBN 978-1-137-31208-2 (eBook)
DOI 10.1057/9781137312082

Library of Congress Cataloging-in-Publication Data

Lewis, Wayne D.
   The politics of parent choice in public education : the choice movement in North Carolina and the United States / Wayne D. Lewis.
      pages cm
   Includes bibliographical references and index.

   1. School choice—North Carolina. 2. Public schools—North Carolina. 3. Education and state—North Carolina. 4. School choice—United States. 5. Public schools—United States. 6. Education and state—United States. I. Title.

LB1027.9.L48 2013
379.1'11—dc23   2013019173

A catalogue record of the book is available from the British Library.

Design by Newgen Knowledge Works (P) Ltd., Chennai, India.

First edition: November 2013

10 9 8 7 6 5 4 3 2 1

*I dedicate this book to the Lewis family: Monica, Maria, Wayne Sr., Gee Jaymee, and Josh Jr.
You all mean the world to me.*

Contents

Acknowledgments   ix

1 Rethinking Public Education   1
2 What Is Choice?   15
3 The Politics of Charter Schools   41
4 The Politics of Charter Schools and Choice in North Carolina   91
5 Busing, Desegregation, and Parent Choice   123
6 Conclusion   143

References   153
Index   165

Acknowledgments

I could not have written this book without the love and unconditional support of my best friend, my life partner, my wife: Monica Nicole Lewis. Thank you for all the things you do to support me. I could not do it without you, and even if I could, I wouldn't want to.

Special thanks to all of my family, friends, and colleagues in Louisiana, North Carolina, and Kentucky. To the Lewis, Dugar, Smith, Sterling, Lawry, Kemp, Wilson, Hills, Watson, Jones, Parks, and Bowman families, to my church families at Greater Power Baptist Church (New Orleans, LA and Rosenburg, TX), Tulane Memorial Baptist Church (New Orleans, LA), St. Paul A. M. E. Church (Raleigh, NC), St. Paul A. M. E. Church (Lexington, KY), and Wesley U. M. C. (Lexington, KY), and last but certainly not least to my brothers of Phi Beta Sigma Fraternity, Inc., I thank all of you for your love, your support, your ears, your stories, your perspectives, your mentoring and guidance, and especially your prayers. Finally, special thank you to my colleagues, friends, and mentors at St. Charles Parish Public Schools (LA), New Orleans Public Schools (LA), Wake County Public Schools (NC), and The University of Kentucky; and to my teachers and professors at St. Augustine High School (New Orleans, LA), Loyola University New Orleans, The University of Akron, The University of New Orleans, and North Carolina State University., The list of individual persons whom I must thank for helping me to get to this place in my career and to write this book is much too long to begin, so please accept my heartfelt thank you to each and every one of you.

1
Rethinking Public Education

Americans like to choose. We like to choose our grocery stores, our dry cleaners, our auto repair shops, our shoe stores, our coffee shops, our restaurants, our places of worship, our doctors, our dentists, and yes, the places our children will go to school. Any number of factors go into making our choices. Kroger is the closest supermarket to my home and I shop there, but not because of its proximity. I am a fan of their organic food line. I drive about 20 miles to my church on Sunday, not because there are no Christian churches closer to my home, but because I enjoy the pastor, congregation, ministries, and music at my church. I frequent a Starbucks coffee shop 15 miles from my home, not because there is not one closer, but because I love the energy there. I take my suits and my shirts to different dry cleaners; one does a great job with my suits, and the other does a better job with my shirts—I like heavy starch. I have chosen to use the same auto repair chain for the last ten years across three states; the service is okay, but more important to me, their prices are competitive and they have high speed Internet—I can work online while I wait for my car to be serviced. I am assured that my choices are in compliance with legal and industry standards. Further, I am personally satisfied with my choices. If at some point I am no longer satisfied, I can choose to go somewhere else.

Saying that parents should be able to choose public schools for their children is pretty controversial in some settings, but it really should not be. Americans have been making school choices for as long as they have been choosing grocery stores. Parents with the means to do so often choose neighborhoods based on schools. Home flyers now frequently list the schools that serve specific neighborhoods. Parents with even greater means, if unsatisfied with the public school serving their neighborhood, can choose to send their children to private or parochial schools or home school their children. Still, other parents use their social and/or political capital to get their children into the public schools that they prefer regardless of the neighborhoods they live in. And just as with grocery stores, parents make school choices for any number of reasons. For some parents, school location is most important. Some parents choose schools for their innovative programs, like language immersion or STEM-focused schools. Some parents choose schools because they like the teachers there. Some parents choose schools based on standardized test scores. Some parents choose schools based on the race and gender composition of the student body and staff. Some parents choose schools based on history or family legacy. Some parents choose schools based on the reputation of athletics or other cocurricular activities for students. The simple answer to why parents choose the schools they do for their children is that there is no simple answer. Just as parents choose shoes and dentists and food products for their children for myriad reasons, the reasons that they choose schools for their children are no fewer.

A simple but unsettling current reality, however, is that all parents do not have the luxury of choosing schools for their children. For many parents, school choices are made for their children by local school districts; and in more cases than not, those boundaries have resulted in children from low-income communities attending schools with fewer resources and less qualified teachers than the schools their more affluent counterparts attend. Parents who live in states and districts with limited or no school choice policies, and who do not have the financial, social, and/or political capital that most middle-class and affluent Americans enjoy, often have no other option than sending their children to district-assigned traditional public schools that may or may not be high quality schools; that may or may not meet their children's unique learning, social, and emotional needs; and that may or may not provide the kind of education they believe to be most appropriate for their children.

In August 2012 I had the opportunity to attend the new student induction ceremony for young men who would be the first students at Carter G. Woodson Academy in Lexington, KY. The academy is a new program grown out of the collaborative efforts of a local church and the Fayette County Public Schools (FCPS). With the explicit mission of preparing young Black men to achieve at high levels, in its inaugural year the program has enrolled students in grades six through nine and promises to offer educational experiences designed to help them realize their full academic potential. Any male student in FCPS may apply to the program. Applications are scored using a rubric and the school uses a tiered lottery system to select students.

The Woodson Academy induction ceremony was one of the most moving events that I have attended for some time, largely because of the excitement of parents about the availability of this unique learning experience designed to meet the needs of their young Black male children. These parents were so excited because few, if any, schools or programs in Kentucky have served Black male students as a group very well. According to data from the Kentucky Department of Education, in the 2010–2011 academic year 53.93% of African American high school students in Kentucky scored at the *Proficient* or *Distinguished* levels in reading on state assessments, and 45.32% scored *Proficient* or *Distinguished* in mathematics compared to their White classmates of whom 74.59% scored *Proficient* or *Distinguished* in reading and 68.79% in mathematics. In FCPS, while higher percentages of African American and White students scored *Proficient* or *Distinguished* in reading and mathematics, greater disparities existed between the percentages of African American and White students scoring *Proficient* or *Distinguished* in reading and mathematics.

Parents attending the Woodson Academy induction ceremony were justifiably excited at having just chosen something new, something different for their children than the traditional public school programs that have not served Black male children well. More traditional public school systems are beginning to think about differentiating schooling approaches to meet children's unique needs. Parents do not care what school type an innovative program is—traditional, magnet, charter, and so on; they care about the availability of school options that meet their children's needs. The creation of programs like the Woodson Academy is long overdue and parents are beginning to demand more options like it. In Lexington, parent demand for the Woodson Academy alone already exceeds the program's capacity.

There is really no question about whether parents want choice; they do. In my work on parent choice and throughout my career in education, I have yet to meet a parent who preferred that someone else choose a school for her child. So yes, parents want to be able choose schools for their children, but without choice policies the most vulnerable families are not able to make choices. The Woodson Academy in Lexington, KY is an example of an innovative program in a traditional public school district, FCPS. The Woodson Academy is not FCPS's only innovative program of choice; they have a few and are busy developing new ones. Few Lexingtonians or Kentuckians would deny that FCPS is one of the more innovative school districts in the state. But with all of its specialized schools and programs, the district is not able to accommodate parent demand for its programs. Hundreds of parents apply for the district's programs every year and are turned away. And because Kentucky has not passed charter school legislation, FCPS is the only show in town. If FCPS does not create it, parents will not have it.

The debate over parent choice policies is about whether choice should be a central tenet of public education in the United States, and whether we will support policies that ensure that all parents have the opportunity to choose high quality schools that meet their children's unique learning needs. More and more parents across the United States are answering those questions saying they want choice to be central to American public education and they want an array of school options available to their children. Parents across the country are saying that all parents should be afforded the right to make school choices for their children, regardless of where they live, their socioeconomic status, their educational attainment, and their children's educational needs.

Reconsidering Public Education and Public Schooling

Serious conversations are underway about what American public education should look like as we move further into the twenty-first century. These are not superficial conversations; instead, they get to the very core of what Americans have known to be public education and public schooling for many generations. One thing that is exciting about these education policy conversations is that they are not just taking place in policy think tanks, government agencies, higher education institutions, and schools. These conversations about what public education should look like and how it should work are happening with and among parents at dinner tables, in coffee shops, at places of worship, in public libraries, in chat rooms, on discussion boards, and on social networking sites. Parents are engaged and in many instances they are driving conversations on education policy, questioning decision-making about how, when, and where children are educated. There are no sacred cows in many of these conversations. Everything is up for debate and reconsideration.

Fundamental to conversations about rethinking public education in the United States is making the distinction between the concept of public education and the system that delivers it (Fuller, 2002). The concept of public education, most fundamentally and succinctly, is the idea that government makes provisions for the people to access education at the public's expense, and ensures that such is adequate and equitable. Throughout the twentieth century and up to the present, the primary manner in which governments in the United States have chosen to provide education for children has been through government-run and regulated schools. Some parents, scholars, and lawmakers are now beginning to question, however, whether government provision of public education should be solely through government-run and government-regulated schools. Some state governments have decided to make provisions for public education in their states through combinations of government-run and regulated schools (traditional public schools), government-regulated-only schools (semiautonomous charter schools), and private schools through the use of tuition vouchers and tax credits for private school tuition and related expenses. I contend that the use of government-regulated-only schools and vouchers and tax credits to provide public education does not change the concept of public education; instead, it only shows the evolution and broadening of governments' approaches and strategies for delivering the best and most appropriate public education in the twenty-first century.

The concept of public schooling must be separated from the concept of public education. Thanks to parent choice policies, there are many more types of public schools available to children now than ever before. These new public school types may not look or feel like the public schools many of us attended, but the examination of three, and only three, critical elements is necessary for determining whether a school is a public one or not. Those areas are access, funding, and accountability (Finn & Gau, 1998; Kolderie, 1990). A public school is one where the public has access to the school, access without a fee. Public schools do not charge students tuition to attend. The requirement of a fee to attend the school, no matter how slight, potentially restricts the access of students on the basis of family wealth. A public school is funded by public sources. This is not to suggest that a public school's funding must be restricted only to public sources, but that the base level of support for educating students is provided by some combination of state, federal, and/or local government funds. Finally, a public school is one that is held accountable for outcomes and/or standards of operation to some government or government-authorized entity. Beyond these areas of access, funding, and accountability, there are any number of varying factors that make public and private schools both similar and different, but none of those additional factors have any bearing on whether a school is a public or a private one.

By those standards, charter schools in every state clearly and comfortably fit within the public school classification. Some critics of this definition charge that it has been custom constructed so that charter schools would fit it. I contend, however, that the standard is constructed relatively broadly to include even the various administrative and organizational arrangements of traditional public schools. For example, as some traditional public schools now contract with private entities to provide school services including management, counseling, therapy, food service, supplemental educational services, and in some cases even primary instruction for students, a definition of public school that required that all school workers be government employees would leave even many of those schools outside of a definition of public schools.

Truthfully, governments' reliance solely on government-run and regulated schools for the provision of public education has never adequately served the needs of many individual families or society writ large. Government-run and regulated schools have served a cross-section of children pretty well, but many children have not been served well by these schools. For generations, children's failure to learn has been placed at their own feet or at the feet of their parents. Only recently is the conversation about education in the United States shifting to where we recognize the limitations of a one-size-fits-all approach to public education, where we send all children through cookie-cutter schools, hoping that everyone gets something out the experience that they can use to build a life and career from. We are now recognizing that children have different learning needs, which to meet appropriately requires different teaching and schooling approaches. We are recognizing that one-size-fits-all schools have never served children with diverse learning and social needs very well. We are also recognizing that families have different preferences for education, reasonable preferences but ones that cannot be accommodated with a one-size-fits-all school model.

The current critical reassessment of public education and public schooling in the United States is overdue. Parents are participating fully in this reassessment and asking tough questions that should have been asked by policy makers and educational leaders long ago; the questions include: Who does the current system serve well and who it does not serve well? Are the current structures best for meeting the needs of an increasingly diverse population of students with diverse needs? Are the current structures best for preparing citizens and workers for the society and economy of tomorrow? Answers to those questions will inform the decisions we make about the future of American public education.

Conversations around what is public about public education are not new, and even the casual education policy observer might recognize that change is afoot regarding the delivery of public education. Miron (2008) writes of a shifting notion of "publicness" in public education, with the question of whether education should be seen as a public or a private good being central to how public education is conceptualized and delivered. Advocates of choice policies have generally emphasized education as a private good, while the traditional public schooling protectorate has emphasized it as a public good; but most scholars including many in the aforementioned camps concede that in reality education rests on a continuum between the two extremes (Labaree, 1997; Lubienski, 2000, 2001, 2003), with clear benefits to the individual student/family, but also recognizable spillover benefits or positive externalities to society at large.

Critics of choice policy argue that any redefinition of public education to include delivery of education through public schools, private schools, and public-private partnerships will move public education further down that public-private goods continuum in the direction of private good. I agree with them; it will move public education further down the continuum. But I believe where public education will likely settle on the continuum will be closer to the middle than the place it has rested throughout most of the twentieth century. If public education is to be regarded as a hybrid of public and private goods, as I believe it should be regarded, then the current dominant conceptualization of public education in the United States, with public funding of education, schooling delivered solely by government-run and regulated schools, and parents having little or no say regarding how, when, or where schooling is delivered is wholly inappropriate. The current dominant conceptualization of public education would only be appropriate if it was a pure public good, but it is not.

While it remains uncertain what American public education and public schooling will look like as we move further into the twenty-first century, it appears highly unlikely that public education will return to a monopoly system, whereby government funds and has complete control over the delivery of public schooling. Parent choice advocates are set on fundamentally changing how public education is defined and delivered, and they will continue to demand that public schools be much more responsive to parents than they have been in the past. For many parent choice advocates, their conviction and beliefs about parent choice are fundamental to who they are as Americans. As Boyd (2007) put it, "Like rust, they will never sleep about the school choice...for it goes to the heart of their beliefs about liberty and the proper role of government" (p. 12). Choice policy advocates face fierce political opposition from teachers unions and their allies, but these reformers will not stop until they have a system in which public education is delivered through a variety of different mechanisms, and where parents choosing schooling options for their children becomes more the norm than the exception to the rule.

Research Methodology

Primary data sources used in this study included interviews with key informants and archival documents. In order to gather descriptive data in informants' own words, the researcher conducted in-depth, semi-structured interviews with 60 study participants. Participants were purposefully sampled, with each participant selected because he or she could "purposefully inform an understanding of the research problem and central phenomenon in the study" (Creswell, 2007, p. 125), and help to facilitate the expansion of theory development (Bogdan & Biklen, 2007. In order to include as broad of a spectrum of responses as possible, informants in this study included parents, journalists, legislators, legislative staff persons, interest group representatives, teachers, school administrators, and state-level education professionals and administrators. Due to the nature of their positions, most participants' email addresses and phone numbers were obtained using the World Wide Web. Parents, however, were identified using a snowball sampling technique as well as through the researcher's personal and professional network. All participants were interviewed individually at their place of employment or office, at their home, or at their children's school. The researcher used an interview protocol for each interview as the use of an interview protocol enables the researcher to collect field notes during the interview and helps the researcher to "organize thoughts on items such as headings, information about starting the interview, concluding ideas, information on ending the interview, and thanking the respondent" (Creswell, 2007, p. 135).

Heeding Bogdan and Biklen's (2007) warning that "when the subject cannot tell his or her story personally in his or her own words, the interview falls out of the qualitative range" (p. 96), the researcher was careful to leave primary and secondary interview questions as open-ended as possible, with the researcher asking study participants about both facts and opinions and soliciting their insights into occurrences. Participants' insights were then used as the basis for future inquiry. Additionally, the researcher asked informants for sources of corroboratory evidence and for assistance with accessing those sources.

Yin (2003) suggests that the researcher has two jobs throughout the interview process: "to follow [his] own line of inquiry, as reflected by [his] study protocol, and (b) to ask [his] actual (conversational) questions in an unbiased manner that also serves the needs of [his] line of inquiry" (Yin, 2003, p. 90). In this study the researcher was interested in uncovering the actions of parents, policy actors, and interest groups in their attempts to influence educational policy. Thus, the researcher pursued this line of inquiry, but all the while he was mindful that in order to be effective, uestioning should be done in a very friendly and nonthreatening way.

The researcher recorded field notes both during and following each interview. Eisenhardt (2002) describes field notes as "an ongoing stream-of-consciousness commentary about what is happening in the research, involving both observation and analysis" (Eisenhardt, 2002, p. 15). The researcher kept a detailed running commentary to himself, writing down whatever impressions occurred. The researcher did not attempt to sift out what *seemed* to be important when recording field notes, as it is often difficult to know what will and will not be useful in research. Instead, he recorded everything he possibly could, and continually asked and forced himself to answer the question, "What am I learning?" (Eisenhardt, 2002, p. 15).

All interviews were audio-recorded using a digital voice recorder. Immediately following each interview, the audio file was downloaded and saved to the researcher's computer. All audio files were then erased from the audio recorder. The interviews were then transcribed verbatim by either the researcher or a paid transcriptionist, and saved as a Microsoft Office document to the researcher's computer. Audio files were then deleted from the researcher's computer.

The researcher also collected over three thousand pages of archival data for analysis including newspaper articles, organizational reports, legislation, legislative statements and other legislative documents, position papers, attorney general opinion letters, issue briefs, State Board of Education policy, emails, agendas from meetings, and information from websites. According to Merriam (1998), the use of documents in qualitative research may be particularly valuable in that documents "do not intrude upon or alter the setting in ways that the presence of the investigator does" (p. 112). Further, Yin (2003) notes that strengths of using archival records in research include their stability, their unobtrusiveness, and their broad coverage. During the interviews, study participants were asked to provide the researcher with any available organizational memos, emails, agendas, research, or opinion papers. Additional organization records were collected from organization websites. Newspaper articles were obtained through Newsbank search databases.

Data Analysis

For both interviews and archival data, the researcher employed the constant comparative method of ongoing data analysis as described by Creswell (2007) and Merriam (1998). The researcher open-coded both interview transcripts and documents for emergent themes and patterns. Open coding involved the researcher examining the data for "salient categories of information" (p. 160). Categories of data were collapsed into a minimal number of themes in order to aid the researcher with developing generalizations and comparing those generalizations with the relevant literature.

Interview transcripts were analyzed with the assistance of Atlas Ti (Scientific Software Development, 2004), a qualitative data analysis software package. This software assisted the researcher with organizing and categorizing data, and facilitating the data's accessibility (Bogdan & Biklen, 2007).

Confirmability and Credibility

Qualitative research does not share the expectation with quantitative research that there will be consistency in the results of different researchers or of the same researcher across time (Bogdan & Biklen, 2007; Merriam, 1998). The meaning of reliability to qualitative researchers centers more on "the fit between what they record as data and what actually occurs in the setting under study" (Bogdan & Biklen, 2003, p. 36). Creswell (2007) notes that the qualitative researcher seeks confirmability rather than objectivity in establishing the value of the data, and these are achieved through an auditing of the research process. To ensure that the reader is able to perform such an audit, all data collection methods and data analysis techniques are made explicit in this methodology section.

Eisner (1991) suggested that instead of using the term validity, which has connotations of quantitative research, qualitative researchers should strive to achieve credibility. According to Eisner (1991), "We seek a confluence of evidence that breeds credibility, that allows us to feel confident about our observations, interpretations, and conclusions" (p. 110). Both Eisner (1991) and Merriam (1998) assert that this type of validity may be achieved by using multiple sources of data. As such, two primary sources of data have been used in this study: interviews and archival documents.

While generalizability is not a primary goal of much of qualitative research, Merriam (2002) contends that when researchers provide thick, rich descriptions of settings and cases, the reader is put in a position to determine whether cases under study are similar to their own. The researcher endeavored to provide such description in this study.

Methodological Limitations

Several limitations result from the researcher's choice of data collection methods. While interviews are an integral component of qualitative research in general, and to this study in particular, there are weaknesses associated with them. There is inevitably a certain amount of bias based on the wording of questions. The researcher attempted to overcome this limitation to the greatest extent possible by soliciting the feedback of colleagues on the interview protocol. Also, whenever interviews are conducted, there is always the possibility that informants will not be completely honest. Yin (2003) refers to this weakness as reflexivity, where the informant gives the interviewer what he or she believes the interviewer wants to hear. The researcher attempted to overcome this limitation by seeking corroboratory and contrary evidence of what informants provided in interviews.

The use of archival records also presents several limitations. Issues of access can prevent the researcher from obtaining records or documents that may be pertinent to the study. The researcher attempted to overcome this limitation by asking informants to assist with access to relevant materials. However, to the extent that certain documents were not obtained, there exists a certain degree of bias in documents. Likewise, documents in and of themselves are subject to varying degrees of bias from their authors. Nevertheless, the researcher believes that by using both interviews and archival documents, the limitations of each method are offset by the strengths of the other.

Author's Statement of Subjectivity

The researcher is an African American man with over ten years of experience in K-12 and higher education. He is a native of New Orleans, LA, and attended predominantly African American Catholic schools in New Orleans from Kindergarten through grade 12, including St. Augustine High School, an all-male historically African American high school that has been lauded locally and nationally for its graduates going on to distinguished careers in politics, business, music, medicine, law, education, and sports. He earned my undergraduate degree at a Catholic university in New Orleans while also working as a deputy with the Orleans Parish Criminal Sheriff's Office and performing as a jazz musician on the weekends. He earned graduate degrees and a certificate from public universities in New Orleans; Akron, OH; and Raleigh, NC. He is married with no children. He is a registered Democrat with moderate political views.

The researcher spent five years as a teacher in traditional public schools in Louisiana and in North Carolina. He entered the teaching profession through a postbaccalaureate teacher preparation program at the University of New Orleans called *Teach Greater New Orleans*. The program was intended to bring nontraditionally trained teachers into public school classrooms in New Orleans and its surrounding areas. Having never attended public schools in New Orleans, he met the challenges of high-needs urban public schools for the first time in 2003 when he accepted his first teaching assignment at Booker T. Washington High School in the New Orleans

Public Schools. Booker T. Washington was at that time the lowest performing high school in the state of Louisiana. After a tumultuous first year of teaching that included the removal of the school's principal and re-staffing of the school, he accepted a position the following year at Albert Cammon Middle School in the nearby high-performing St. Charles Parish Public Schools. He taught in St. Charles Parish until 2005 when Hurricane Katrina devastated the city of New Orleans and the Louisiana and Mississippi Gulf Coast.

Following Hurricane Katrina, he and his wife relocated to accept teaching positions in the Wake County Public Schools in North Carolina. For the next three years he taught at Longview School in Raleigh, NC, a public-separate school serving children with severe emotional and behavior disturbance. In 2006 while still teaching at Longview, he decided to pursue doctoral studies at North Carolina State University. In 2008 he made the decision to leave K-12 teaching to pursue full-time doctoral study, research, and to teach at the undergraduate level preparing aspiring teachers. After completing doctoral study, he accepted a position as an assistant professor in the College of Education at the University of Kentucky where he remains today, teaching in the areas of education politics and policy, school-community collaboration, human resources management, and diversity.

The researcher has have held memberships in several teacher unions/professional associations. While teaching in Louisiana he was a member of the United Teachers of New Orleans (UTNO), an AFT (American Federation of Teachers) affiliate organization that collectively bargained with the Orleans Parish School Board. While teaching in North Carolina he was a member of North Carolina Association of Educators (NCAE), an affiliate of the National Education Association (NEA), and Professional Educators of North Carolina (PENC). Since his first days as a teacher in the New Orleans Public Schools he has been interested in public school reform. My specific interest in school choice reform began while a graduate student at North Carolina State University. In Kentucky for the last three years, he has worked with the Black Alliance for Educational Options (BAEO) and other groups in attempts to pass parent choice policies in the state legislature. Additionally, he serves on the board of the Kentucky Charter School Association, a Louisville-based nonprofit organization that supports the passage of charter school legislation in Kentucky.

Epistemological Position

This study is conducted from a realist epistemological position. According to Gutek (2004), realism "asserts that we live in a world of objects that truly exist and are external to us. Although objects exist outside of us, we can acquire information about them and come to know them" (p. 35). However, in this study, as any study conducted from a realist position, the data collection and analysis employed are only an attempt to directly observe that objective reality. A realist stance, while supposing that objective reality exists beyond our experiences, recognizes that we also need our creative minds to clarify its existence and then to identify explanatory mechanisms (Grbich, 2007). Thus, the researcher's role in this study was to collect, analyze, and present data in such a manner that both the researcher and reader might be able to draw conclusions and come as close as possible to observing reality as it truly exists.

Final Thoughts

Parents' advocacy for policy change leading to expanded school options for families centers on a desire to have public schools more directly accountable and responsive to parents' individual needs and/or desires as opposed to the current standard of public schools being held only *accountable to* elected leaders, bodies, or bureaucratic entities, and *accountable for* meeting government designated standards. The current dominant conceptualization of public education holds that the combination of public funding, government-employed workers, and governmental regulation and accountability are what make public schools public. But parent choice advocates challenge one, some, or most of those notions. For example, underlying many parents' advocacy for school voucher and tuition tax credit policies is their desire to have significantly greater control over where their children attend school, and to have schools held more directly accountable to parents through a competitive public and private education marketplace. The implications of this and other choice-related policy changes are far-reaching. My hope is that this book will serve as a resource for parents, educators, and educational researchers who wish to better understand (a) the parent choice policy ideas being debated around the country, (b) the political dynamics surrounding those debates, and (c) what parent choice advocates across the country are continuing to push for and what the implications of their proposed changes might be.

2

What Is Choice?

By most accounts, the modern school choice movement can be traced back to the 1980s with the US Supreme Court setting a significant precedent with its decision in *Mueller v. Allen* in 1983 (Kafer, 2009). The plaintiffs in the case had challenged a Minnesota statue, which allowed for a state education tax deduction for independent school expenses, on the grounds that it violated the Establishment Clause of the US Constitution. The district court sided with the state, ruling that the law was "neutral on its face and in its application and does not have a primary effect of either advancing or inhibiting religion." The Eighth Circuit Court of Appeals and eventually the US Supreme Court upheld the district court's decision. Minnesota then continued to push the choice envelope by enacting the first statewide interdistrict public school choice law allowing students to transfer from their assigned public schools to public schools in other school districts. Then in 1987, Iowa enacted a law allowing families that earned less than $45,000 annually to deduct up to $1,000 per child annually from their state income tax liability for education expenses.

In the 1990s, the first modern school voucher program for low-income students was established in Milwaukee. More than 23 thousand children from low-income families participated in the Milwaukee Parental Choice Program using vouchers to attend independent schools in 2012. In 1991, Minnesota became the first state in the United States to pass legislation allowing the creation of charter schools. Minnesota law defines charter schools as public schools of choice run by teachers, parents, community leaders, or other groups, operating under a charter agreement between that group and a state charter authorizer. In 1997, Minnesota made school choice history again, enacting a law allowing low- and middle-income families a refundable tax credit for education expenses, excluding tuition. That law also raised the maximum deduction for elementary school expenses—including tuition—to $1,625, and raised the limit to $2,500 for middle and high school expenses. Also in

1997, Arizona passed a law allowing individuals to take a tax credit up to $500 for donations to organizations providing scholarships for students to attend private schools; and a tax credit up to $200 for donations to public school extracurricular activities (Kafer, 2009). The nation's first statewide voucher programs came in 1999 with Florida's passage of legislation creating its Opportunity Scholarships for students attending persistently failing schools and its McKay Scholarships for students with disabilities (McCarthy, 2000). While the Opportunity Scholarships Program was eventually struck down with courts finding that it violated the Florida Constitution, the McKay Scholarship Program continues to operate and serves over 20 thousand students across the state.

These passages of policy in the states have been milestones for the national parent choice movement. But behind each of these events, there are stories; stories of politics, policy details, advocacy, and opposition. The purpose of this chapter is to unpack these stories for the reader, providing a general framework for understanding both the language and landscape of parent choice policies and the politics surrounding them. This chapter is not intended to bring the reader to the level of choice policy expert, but to provide her with a basic understanding of choice reform policies, make her aware of the variation in such policies across the states, and provide context for choice policy advocacy and opposition.

The Choice Advocacy Landscape

Any treatment of the politics of the parent choice movement would be remiss if it did not highlight the important role that advocacy organizations have played in the organization and mobilization parent and community choice policy advocates. In each state where choice policy has been expanded and even in states where it has not, there are any number of state and local advocacy organizations that have figured prominently in choice policy debates. While charting and discussing all of those organizations is beyond the scope of this work, I do wish to highlight a few of the large advocacy organizations whose work has been central to advancing choice at both the national and state levels.

To begin, any list of such organizations would have to include the National Alliance for Public Charter Schools as the leading force for expanding and strengthening charter school policies in the United States. The Alliance grew out of the former Charter School Leaders Council. It was founded in 2004 for the purpose of serving as the national umbrella organization for state and local charter school advocacy efforts (DeBray-Pelot, Lubienski, & Scott, 2007). The Alliance has become the dominant charter school advocacy organization in the United States. The organization's mission is "to lead public education to unprecedented levels of academic achievement for all students by fostering a strong charter sector." The Alliance's functions include providing assistance to state charter school advocacy organizations, and developing and advocating for educational policy that leads to the creation and support of high-quality charter schools. The Alliance is the leading clearinghouse for information on charter school policy and performance, and it also serves as a clearinghouse for parents seeking information on charter schools. The Alliance's national conference is the largest meeting of charter school advocates, supporters, parents, educators, and researchers in the country. Funders for the Alliance have included the Walton Family, Gates, Annie E. Casey, Pisces, and Fordham Foundations (DeBray-Pelot et al., 2007).

The Black Alliance for Educational Options (BAEO) is at the top of the list of organizations that have worked to organize and grow the movement for parent choice in communities of color. BAEO grew out of a March 1999 meeting of the Institute for the Transformation of Learning at Marquette University in Milwaukee, WI, where participants voiced concern over the lack of quality educational options for Blacks. That group expressed a desire to have a national organization to lead the fight for expanding education options available to Blacks. In response to that call, BAEO was founded in December 1999 in Washington DC by 50 Black leaders. Dr. Howard Fuller was elected president of the organization's 29-member board of directors. Fuller was a longtime community activist, and had an impressive resume of leadership and administrative posts, including dean of the Milwaukee Area Technical College, director of the Milwaukee Department of Health and Human Services, superintendent of the Milwaukee Public Schools, and director of the Institute for the Transformation of Learning at Marquette University.

BAEO has become the nation's leading advocate for expanding school options for Black families. The organization's mission is explicitly to "increase access to high-quality educational options for Black children by actively supporting parental choice policies and programs that empower low-income and working-class Black families." BAEO's mission is rooted in the belief that "all parents ought to have the capacity to choose the learning environments that they believe are best for their children" (Fuller, 2002, p. 3). BAEO seeks a "radical alteration of urban schools as a means to educate African American students" (DeBray-Pelot et al., 2007), with choice as the centerpiece of that reform. For BAEO, choice means "policies that give families the capacity to choose from a wide range of learning environments they feel are best for their children" (Fuller, 2002, p. 3), with those options including traditional public schools, magnet schools, charter schools, public/private partnerships, supplemental education programs, cyber schools, Black independent schools, and innovative educational programs and practices (Fuller, 2002). BAEO has actively supported the expansion of school options for low-income Black families in the District of Columbia, Alabama, Kentucky, Louisiana, Missouri, Mississippi, Ohio, and Pennsylvania; engaging in activities including parent and community education and mobilization, supporting candidates for office, and other grassroots advocacy work (DeBray-Pelot et al., 2007). BAEO's funders have included the Bradley Foundation, the Walton Family Foundation, the Milton and Rose D. Friedman Foundation, and the American Education Reform Council.

The Hispanic Council for Reform and Educational Options (CREO) is the nation's only Hispanic national advocacy organization dedicated to K-12 education reform. It was founded in 2001 in response to the troubling educational outcomes for Hispanic children in the United States. Hispanic CREO was formed expressly to provide parents with information and resources for advocating for their children, and it supports a range of choice options for parents including but not limited to high-quality traditional public schools, magnet schools, charter schools, home schooling, and private schools. The organization's mission is "to create awareness of the educational crisis that exists within the Hispanic community nationally by empowering Hispanic parent to become advocates for their children. Hispanic CREO believes that education is a civil right for every child in the United States. The organization's grassroots and advocacy work have been focused in Texas, Florida, Arizona, Colorado, and New Jersey. In those states it works indirectly to influence policy through the sharing of information, data, and statistics, and through publicity using its large network of parents, contacting local media, and organizing parent rallies (DeBray-Pelot et al., 2007; Scott, Lubienski, & DeBray-Pelot, 2009). Hispanic CREO's efforts have been supported by funding from the Bradley, Walton, and Daniel Foundations (DeBray-Pelot et al., 2007).

State-level advocacy organizations have also figured very prominently in state-level choice policy debates. One such state organization that has played a major role in the creation and expansion of choice policies is Parents for Educational Freedom in North Carolina (PEFNC). PEFNC is a statewide organization that supports the expansion of choice for parents in North Carolina. The organization's mission is "to inform parents of the benefits of expanded educational options and empower them to exercise freedom in meeting their children's needs, regardless of race, national origin, income or religion." For PEFNC, choice means "allowing parents to send their children to their school of choice—public, private, or nontraditional—regardless of address or income." The group has been instrumental in the passage of charter school legislation in North Carolina in 1996, the elimination of the state's charter school cap in 2011, and the 2011 passage of legislation that gives tax credits to parents of children with special needs for educational expenses at private schools. At the time of this book's writing, PEFNC was leading advocacy in North Carolina for passage of a bill that would create a North Carolina Opportunity Scholarship Tax Credit Program, whereby corporations would receive a state tax credit for contributions to nonprofit scholarship granting organizations.

The remainder of this chapter spends time fleshing out the policies that these advocacy organizations have pushed for, both at the federal and state levels. The following discussion includes definitions of the most commonly pursued choice measures, discussion of the politics surrounding the push for passage and expansion of policies, and discussion of past and ongoing legal challenges of choice policies in the states.

Charter Schools

Charter schools are a state-level education reform, and as such, significant variations exist with both individual charter schools and the state legislation that authorizes them. Those variations limit the extent to which generalizations may be made about charter schools across the United States. What can be said broadly of the charter school concept is that it is grounded in site-based management theory, which espouses that budgeting, human resources, curriculum, and instructional decisions are better made at the school level (Cheng, 1996; Chubb & Moe, 1988; Nathan, 1996; Vergari, 2007). Thus, charter schools in most states are freed from varying degrees of regulations that traditional public schools are subject to. Charter schools' greater degree of autonomy comes at the price of increased academic accountability, but the structure and workings of charter school accountability frameworks vary considerably by state. In some states charter schools are held accountable to their authorizing boards, other states hold charter schools accountable to parents through the education marketplace (if a charter school does not attract a sufficient number of students, it is forced to close), and others use combinations of performance-based, market-based, and bureaucratic accountability systems. Both the accountability for results and site-based management tenets of charter school reform represent a fundamental shift in the way Americans think about public education (Fusarelli, 2001).

As of 2012, 41 states and the District of Columbia had enacted some form of charter school legislation, with over 5,700 schools serving nearly

2 million students. Charter schools have been the most widespread school choice reform. Charter schools are seen as much less controversial than voucher or tax credit programs, and in some states, including North Carolina, the passage of charter school legislation has been seen by the traditional public school protectorate as the acceptance of the lesser of the parent choice evils. This is not to suggest, however, that charter schools have been free from legal challenges or that the passage of charter school legislation in most states has come easily. While charter schools are less controversial than vouchers, they have not been welcomed by teachers unions and their allies in most states. Although charter school legislation now exists in 41 states and the District of Columbia, charter schools continue to face challenges related to expansion and funding; and in most states that have not adopted charter school legislation, opponents of parent choice reforms continue to fight mightily to keep charters schools out of states where there are currently none.

A more in-depth discussion of charter school reform and the politics of the charter school reform model is included in chapter 3.

Magnet Schools

Magnet schools were devised initially as a strategy for racially integrating schools. Magnets schools have provided parents an alternative to district-assigned traditional public schools, and to school districts an alternative to busing for achieving racial balance in schools (Goldring & Smrekar, 2002). As their name implies, magnets were intended to attract students from all over school districts with their thematic or content-specific curricula, such as math and science, computers and technology, engineering, or healthcare professions. Because there are typically many more applications than available seats in magnets, most schools use a lottery for admission, while others use a first-come first-served approach, and some schools use a selective admissions approach involving the use of achievement testing (Goldring & Smrekar, 2002). Most magnets have been established in relatively large urban school districts, and in some of those districts significant portions of districts' students are served by magnet schools, and in the vast majority of districts with magnet schools there is a much higher demand for magnet schools than districts can accommodate, resulting in long waiting lists (Goldring & Smrekar, 2000, 2002).

The federal Magnet Schools Assistance Program (MSAP), a grant program of the *Elementary and Secondary Education Act*, has played a significant role in the creation and expansion of magnet schools. MSAP is intended to support school districts in efforts to eliminate, reduce, or prevent the isolation of students of color in schools. MSAP provides grants to eligible school districts for the purpose of establishing or maintaining magnet schools under a court-ordered or federally approved voluntary school desegregation plan.

In addition to helping to racially desegregate schools, the theory behind the creation of magnet schools, as with other choice policy measures, is that allowing parents to choose schools for their children creates market-like pressure for schools. Schools that are chosen continue to respond to parents and children's needs and desires, while schools that are not chosen are forced to improve, do a better job of responding to parents' needs and desires, or close. Specifically in the case of magnet schools, if a school fails to attract applicants from across the district or if parents become dissatisfied with their children's educational experience, parents may disenroll their children and send them elsewhere, forcing the school to change.

Today, while magnet schools continue to serve the purpose of attracting more affluent, suburban children into predominantly minority central city schools, districts are at the drawing board thinking of new purposes for magnets as well. The good news for school districts is that parent interest in magnets has remained high. Parents' increased demands for more school options for their children and court rulings that signal the end of the use of race as a factor in student assignment plans, are requiring educational leaders to think beyond the traditional use of magnets. Examples include some districts transforming all of their traditional public schools into magnet schools in an effort to greatly expand the school options available to parents, and other districts working to blend characteristics of traditional neighborhood schools with magnet schools.

Interdistrict and Intradistrict Choice Policies

While charter school and school voucher policies consume much of the national conversation on parent choice policies, inter- and intradistrict choice policies are more widely used choice policies in the states (Godwin, Leland, Baxter, & Southworth, 2006), and for choice advocates, these policies have the benefits of providing families with additional school options while being less politically controversial. These policies, as other choice policies, are intended to provide students attending persistently low-performing schools the option of transferring to a better performing school (Ni & Arsen, 2011). Intradistrict choice policies are typically district choice policies that allow families to choose among some or all of the schools within a given school district. One example of an intradistrict choice policy is the Jefferson County Public Schools (Louisville, KY) student assignment plan that based on students' addresses, gives them both an initial school assignment as well as other specific school options including magnet schools based on availability and other factors (McNeal, 2009).

Interdistrict choice policies are typically state policies that allow students to transfer to schools both within their school district and to schools in other school districts. These state policies vary considerably in terms of which students are eligible for such transfers, the requirements for districts receiving students from neighboring school districts, and how funding follows students from their school district of residence to their district of choice. One example of an interdistrict choice policy is Michigan's interdistrict choice policy passed in 1996, three years after the passage of the state's charter school policy. The policy, known in Michigan as the *schools of choice* program, lets each school district in the state decide whether it will admit students from other districts and specify how many students it will admit by school and by grade level. Districts may also decide whether transferring students must reside within the district's county. A district may not prohibit students residing within its attendance boundaries from transferring to another school district, but districts are not required to provide transportation for students transferring to other districts. Participation in Michigan's interdistrict choice policy has been higher than in other states with similar policies.

In addition to providing students attending low-performing schools other school options, the rationale behind interdistrict choice policies, and in fact behind the introduction of market mechanisms into public education generally, is that poorly performing schools' loss of funding due to student transfer spurs low-performing schools to improve in order to retain students; improvement which ultimately will benefit students who remain in the school (Chubb & Moe, 1990; Fiske & Ladd, 2000; Hoxby, 2003; Peterson & Hassel, 1998). That logic model only holds true, however, when student transfer under interdistrict choice policies is indeed based on school effectiveness and not based on other social and environmental factors including the demographic profile of the school's student body. Questions remain regarding whether in fact the market pressures placed on schools due to participation in interdistrict choice programs is based solely on school effectiveness and not as a result of parents seeking more racially and socioeconomically homogeneous school settings. In Michigan, for example, Ni and Arsen (2011) found that school effectiveness had no systematic influence on parents' participation in interdistrict transfer, but that schools' loss of students due to transfers was significantly higher in districts serving high percentages of low-income students. Ni and Arsen's findings raise important questions about the market pressures placed on schools as a result of interdistrict choice, including whether an effective school could potentially face *unjust* market pressure—pressure to change the demographic profile of its student body instead of pressure to improve performance. Additionally, concerns are raised regarding whether interdistrict choice policies might place an *unjust* financial burden on districts simply because of the demographic profile of the students it serves.

School Voucher Programs

Programs that provide publicly funded vouchers to families for students to attend private schools are the most controversial of the current parent choice policy measures in the United States. (Boyd, 2007; Fuller, 2000; McCarthy, 2000). Publicly funded school voucher programs are not to be confused with privately funded scholarship programs that provide limited numbers of students with vouchers or scholarships to cover part or all of the cost of tuition at private schools. Privately funded scholarship programs now exist in states across the country. The first privately funded voucher program in the United States, the Educational CHOICE Charitable Trust, began in 1991. Programs such as Educational CHOICE and the Children's Scholarship Fund (CSF) have now provided over 100 thousand scholarships to low-income families in cities across the United States.

Voucher advocates and opponents disagree on just about everything, with one exception; both camps agree that if voucher reforms were adopted on a large scale, public education in the United States would be changed in dramatic fashion (McCarthy, 2000). Making the debate even more contentious is the reality that many proponents of choice do not support the passage of universal voucher policies. For example, great numbers of charter school supporters do not support policies that would result in public funds supporting private and religious schools. Opponents of voucher policies view the policy measure as the beginning of a movement to completely privatize public education in the United States. Such a perception is not unwarranted as some voucher proponents do advocate for a complete reconceptualization of public education, including the expansion of voucher programs in the states beyond low-income students and students with special needs.

The origin of the school voucher concept is attributed to Milton Friedman (1955), who made the assertion that public schooling in the

United States was so inefficient and incapable of preparing learners across the ability spectrum for careers and college that the only way to bring about significant improvement in public education was through privatization, with the majority of learners receiving their schooling through private enterprises. In more recent work, Friedman (1997) continued to assert that "a voucher system that would enable parents to choose freely the schools that their children attend is the most feasible way to improve elementary and secondary education in the US" (p. 341). According to Friedman (1997):

> Such a voucher system will encourage privatization of a sizeable fraction of educational services. That will unleash the drive, imagination and energy of competitive free enterprise to revolutionize the education process. The competition will force government schools to improve in order to retain their clientele. Except for a small group who have a vested interest in the present system, everyone would win: parents, students, teachers, taxpayers, private entrepreneurs and, above all, the residents of the central cities. (p. 341)

Friedman believed that only the delivery of schooling through private enterprises and forcing traditional public schools to compete with private providers to keep their clientele would bring about the necessary improvement in traditional public schools.

Earlier research on the effectiveness of privately funded voucher programs gave reason for cautious optimism for school vouchers and fueled the expansion of voucher programs into the public domain. Greene (2001) tested the effects of the Children's Scholarship Fund Program in Charlotte, NC. Children in the study were enrolled in grades 2 through 8 and were grouped into one of three categories: (a) *choice students*—those who won a scholarship and enrolled in a private school, (b) *noncomplying students*—those who won a scholarship but either remained in a public school or moved out of the area, or (c) *control students*—those who did not win a scholarship. Choice students, chosen by lottery, were awarded scholarship up to $1,700 to go toward the cost of tuition expenses at a private school of the family's choice. Using a randomized control design, the study showed that after one year, choice students scored 5.9 percentile points higher in math on the Iowa Test of Basic Skills (ITBS) than comparable students who remained in public schools, and 6.5 percentile points higher than their public school counterparts in reading. "On average, a scholarship raised students from the 30th percentile to the 37th percentile" (Greene, 2001, p. 57).

Similarly, an evaluation of the Washington Scholarship Fund (WSF), a privately funded school voucher program in Washington, DC, showed significant academic gains for students who used the scholarships to escape their troubled public schools and enroll in private schools. Specifically, Wolf, Peterson, and West (2001) found that after two years of operation, African American students who switched to private schools scored 9 national percentile rank (NPR) points higher their public school peers in combined reading and mathematics achievement. African American students in Wolf et al.'s study scored an average of 8 NPR points higher in reading and 10 NPR points higher in mathematics than students in the study's control group. Interestingly, however, no significant test score differences between voucher users and the control group were observed for the small number of non–African American students in the evaluation.

As with other state-level education reforms, and the details of school voucher programs vary; in fact, the details of voucher programs may vary even more than the details of other state-level choice policies. What follows is description and discussion of a few current publicly funded school voucher programs.

Milwaukee, WI

The impetus for major choice policy reform in Milwaukee can be traced back to 1976, when a federal court found that African American children in Milwaukee were unlawfully confined to segregated schools (Fuller, 2000). That ruling resulted in the local school district developing a desegregation plan; a staple of which was busing disproportionate numbers of students of color and low-income students to schools often distant from their homes (Fuller, 2000). By most accounts, that plan resulted in the *successful* desegregation of the city's schools. But a closer look at the plan revealed a few ugly truths about the busing plan. The plan had (a) intentionally provided more and better school options to White parents and (b) intentionally limited the number of White children who would be forced to travel to distant schools, placing the greater burden of busing on Black families (Fuller, 1985, 2000; Mitchell, 1989). In 1999, a former Milwaukee school official made news when he admitted that *White benefit* was in fact a central consideration during the development of the busing plan (Fuller, 1985, 2000). But in addition to the now confirmed disproportionate burden placed on Black families by the district's busing plan, by the mid-1980s, even with school desegregation, and despite attempts by the school district to distort the achievement of Black students, standardized test scores showed that the majority of Milwaukee's Black children in all grade levels and in most subjects scored well below the fiftieth percentile (Fuller, 1985, 2000).

These findings along with the long-standing disenchantment of Milwaukee's Black community with the public school system gave rise to a coalition that would push for major educational reform. That coalition's push was instrumental in the passage and enactment of the Milwaukee Parental Choice Program in 1990, the nation's first modern school voucher program for low-income students (Kafer, 2009; Fuller, 2000; McCarthy, 2000). The enabling legislation was sponsored by Rep. Polly Williams (D), a longtime African American community activist in Milwaukee, and Republican governor Tommy Thompson. The program initially provided to a limited number of low-income parents, vouchers that could be used to pay tuition and fees at nonreligious private schools.

During the 1994 Wisconsin elections, a bipartisan coalition of parents, employers, and civic leaders exerted considerable pressure on candidates to expand the program; and in 1995, Wisconsin governor Tommy Thompson proposed that the program be expanded to include all low-income families in the Milwaukee Public Schools. Thompson's proposal was amended in the legislature, but he and the parent coalition did manage to get legislation passed that significantly expanded the voucher program. That new legislation expanded the program by adding religious schools as options for parents, but it capped participation in the program at 15% of the Milwaukee Public Schools, which then was approximately 16 thousand families. During the program's first decade of operation, participation increased from three hundred students in the program's first year to nearly eight thousand students during the 1999–2000 academic term (Fuller, 2000).

With the voucher program's expansion to include religious schools, the local teachers union filed suit contesting the program on the grounds that it violated both the Establishment Clause of the US Constitution and the Wisconsin Constitution (Kafer, 2009). Those suits were unsuccessful. In 1998, the voucher program was upheld by the Wisconsin Supreme Court with the court holding that it neither violated the Establishment Clause because the program's purpose was secular, nor did it advance religion or create an "excessive entanglement" between the state and religious institutions. Regarding provisions of the Wisconsin Constitution that state no person should be compelled to support religious institutions nor any state funds be used for religious societies or religious or theological seminaries, the court ruled that

> public funds may be placed at the disposal of third parties so long as the program on its face is neutral between sectarian and nonsectarian alternatives and the transmission of funds is guided by the independent decisions of third parties...and that public funds generally may be provided to

sectarian educational institutions so long as steps are taken not to subsidize religious functions. (*Jackson v. Benson*, 578 N.W.2d 602 [Wisc. 1998])

In 2012, more than 23 thousand students from low-income families participated in the Milwaukee Parental Choice Program, using vouchers to attend independent schools.

Witte, Sterr, and Thorn's (1995) analysis of student achievement data and interviews with families participating in the Milwaukee school voucher program during the 1990s showed the following of the program:

- Over its first five years, most participating students were Black or Hispanic, from very low-income families, from homes where parents were not married, and achieving at considerably lower levels than the average Milwaukee Public Schools student.
- Parents participating in the program reported much greater levels of satisfaction with their Choice private schools than with the Milwaukee Public School their children previously attended; and parents reported significantly higher levels of involvement in Choice schools than in their children's previous Milwaukee Public School.
- Generally, results showed no substantial difference over the life of the program between students participating in the voucher program and Milwaukee Public School students.

Cleveland, OH

In response to years of persistently low-achieving schools in Cleveland, a federal district court placed the Cleveland City Schools under control of the Ohio State Superintendent of Public Instruction. The Court deemed the school district as having been "mismanaged by the local school board" (Weisenberger, 2001, p. 565). Part of the superintendent's plan for reform in Cleveland was the creation of Ohio's Pilot Project Scholarship Program. The program was designed to funnel funding to parents in two ways. First, a voucher was provided to parents to pay for 90% of the cost of tuition up to $2,250 at a participating public or private school in Cleveland or its surrounding suburbs. Families in Cleveland with incomes below 200% of the poverty line are given priority. Second, grants were provided to students in Cleveland public schools to pay for tutoring services. Students from low-income families are eligible to receive 90% of the cost of services up to $360, and other students are eligible to receive up to 75% of that cost.

Private schools and public schools in adjacent school districts could apply to participate in the scholarship program. Schools that desired to participate in the program were required to register and meet the program's eligibility requirements, including nondiscriminatory placement of students and "a prohibition on teaching hatred of or biases against any religious, racial, or ethnic group" (Weisenberger, 2001, p. 565). The program's payments came in the form of checks made out to and issued to parents. Parents would then endorse the check over to the chosen private school. The program required that participating private schools cap their tuition at $2,500 per student. If a parent chose to send their child to a participating public school the check would be made out to and issued to the participating school district instead of the parent.

The constitutionality of the Cleveland voucher program was challenged in court by the Ohio Federation of Teachers on the grounds that it violated both the Establishment Clause of the US Constitution and the Ohio state constitution. After years of litigation and back-and-forth rulings all the way through the court system, the US Supreme Court's ruling in *Zelman v. Simmons-Harris* in 1992 put to rest—at least for now—any questions about whether the Cleveland voucher program or any similar programs are in violation of the Establishment Clause of the US Constitution. Ultimately, in a 5–4 divided decision with Justices Rehnquist, Kennedy, O'Connor, Scalia, and Thomas in the majority, and Justices Stevens, Souter, Ginsburg, and Breyer dissenting, the US Supreme Court found Ohio's Pilot Project Scholarship Program to be "neutral with respect to religion, and an exercise of genuine choice for the parents" (Eberle-Peay, 2012, p. 710), since state funds were directed first to parents who could then choose whether to use the funds at a sectarian school. The Court majority completely rejected the plaintiff's argument that the program violated the Establishment Clause by providing families with a financial incentive to attend a religious school on the grounds that families participating in the program had the options of sending their children to a community school, magnet school, or traditional public school at no cost at all (Liekweg, 2004). Liekweg (2004) provided the following analysis of the Court's majority opinion in *Zelman*:

> To support its conclusion that the Cleveland voucher program was a true private choice program, and thus constitutional, the Court noted several aspects about the program, such as it (1) was neutral in all respects towards religion, (2) was part of a general and multifaceted undertaking by the State to provide educational opportunities, (3) conferred assistance to a broad class of individuals defined without reference to religion, and (4) permits the participation of all religious and nonreligious private schools in Cleveland, as well as adjacent public schools.... Any objective observer

familiar with the full history and context of the Cleveland program would, in the Court's view, reasonably see it as one aspect of a broader undertaking to assist poor children in failed schools, not as an endorsement of religious schooling in general. (p. 52)

The US Supreme Court's ruling in Zelman, however, has not stopped challenges to voucher programs on the basis of violations to state constitutions. According to Liekweg (2004), "By upholding the constitutionality of the Cleveland voucher program, the Court has basically taken the Federal Establishment Clause issue out of the public debate over school choice" (p. 55), but "the debate over school choice programs will continue into the foreseeable future" (p. 56), with most litigation shifting now to arguing over state constitutional provisions. This has indeed been the case as voucher programs in Florida, Arizona, and New Hampshire have been thrown out or significantly revised based on state courts rulings that the direction of public monies to sectarian schools, whether or not parents were the ones making the choice of school, was a violation of state constitutions or statutes (Eberle-Peay, 2012).

Washington DC

In 2004 President George W. Bush signed the D.C. School Choice Incentive Act into law that provided $14 million in funding to create the DC Opportunity Scholarship Program (OSP), providing approximately 1,700 scholarship to students from low-income families in DC and becoming the nation's first federally funded voucher or scholarship program. The US secretary of Education and the mayor of DC selected the Washington Scholarship Fund (WSF) and its partners, who already funded and administered a privately funded scholarship program in DC, to administer the new federally funded program. Scholarship-eligible students include those whose families have an annual household income below 185% of the poverty level, which in 2007 was approximately $37,000 per year for a family of four. Students selected for the program receive scholarships worth up to $7,500 to pay for tuition, fees, and transportation expenses at a participating nonpublic elementary or secondary school of the parents' choice in DC. The scholarships may be renewed for up to five years, providing that families continue to meet eligibility requirements for the program and students remain in good academic standing at the school. In its first year of program implementation, over one thousand students (75% of the total number of scholarships awarded) used the scholarship to attend a private school (Stewart, Wolf, & Cornman, 2005, 2007).

The future of the OSP looked bleak in 2008. The newly elected Democratic Congress made the decision to eliminate the federally funded voucher program. The program's constituents and proponents turned out in large numbers to protest the decision. Parent protest resulted in President Obama offering a compromise measure: funding would continue for the program's then-current students, but no additional students would be accepted into the program. In 2011, Congress passed the Scholarships for Opportunity and Results (SOAR) Act, championed by Republican House Speaker John Boehner and Senate Independent Joe Lieberman, which restored funding to the program and expanded it to 1,615 slots. Then after several years of attack by Congressional Republican parent choice advocates and parent advocates for expanded choice in DC, the Obama administration softened its stance on the program further and in 2012 reached an agreement with John Boehner and the Republican House to fund an additional 85 slots for the voucher program, bringing the number of children served by the program to 1,700.

Some research has quantitatively assessed the effectiveness of the OSP in DC. But equally as important as research that evaluates gains or declines in student achievement for voucher programs, are the voices of families and students who have received and used vouchers to exit public schools and attend private schools of their choosing. While rigorous quantitative analysis of test scores, achievement, discipline and safety data, and student transfer is necessary to inform the education policy conversation, "quantitative evaluations necessarily abstract from the contextual nuance of what is happening in the lives of the families experiencing the program" (Stewart et al., 2007, p. 313). In response to a lack of understanding how the DC program impacted families, Stewart et al. (2005, 2007) set out to capture those missing voices; the voices of parents and students. Informed by focus group discussions and personal interviews, the researchers found that after the first year of implementation of the DC OSP most parents showed gratitude for the program and saw the OSP as an opportunity to access higher quality educational options for their children than they would have been capable of accessing without the scholarship. Parents commonly reported that they had applied to the OSP because "they thought choice would allow them to obtain a better education for their child" and, "they believed private schools would have less violence and stricter discipline than the public schools" (Stewart et al., 2007, p. 327). Few of the parents interviewed reported having explored other school choice options; and most parents first learned of the OSP through the program's marketing and outreach efforts, which included mailings and fliers, word of mouth, and advertisements in newspapers, on buses, and on television and the radio.

The researchers found that students, particularly students in middle grades, saw the OSP as "help[ing] them avoid undesirable educational situations and improved their chances of success" (Stewart et al., 2007, p. 325). According to Stewart et al., (2007), students' responses suggested that they saw OSP as an opportunity to have greater educational opportunities, and that they were somewhat frustrated and dissatisfied with their past school experiences. One middle school student succinctly stated, "It helps us get into a better school to help us learn more" (Stewart et al., 2007, p. 325). Another middle school student put it this way:

> It gave you a way out of nowhere. You're not used to being on top of everything, or you're not the person—you're not the one that got the killer jump shot—but you're still trying to go somewhere and go to school and get away from this environment and you've got that opportunity to use your scholarship. (Stewart et al., 2007, p. 328)

Florida

Florida has enacted two statewide school voucher programs. The Florida Opportunity Scholars Program, the first statewide school choice program in the United States, was enacted to provide tuition vouchers for students in persistently failing schools. Enacted in 1999, by 2006 the program was serving hundreds of students across the state, with African American and Hispanic students making up 95% of scholarship recipients (Knepper, 2006). But in 2006, after legal challenges to the program by Florida teachers unions, the program was struck down by the Florida Supreme Court on the grounds that it violated the "uniformity clause" of the Florida Constitution, which guarantees that all students will have a "*uniform*, efficient, safe, secure, and high quality school system of free public schools."

The McKay Scholarship Program, also enacted in 1999 in Florida, provides tuition vouchers for students with disabilities. Voucher programs for students with special needs have been enacted across the country in states including Georgia, Louisiana, Oklahoma, Ohio, and Utah; but the McKay Program was the first and continues to be the largest such program in the country. The statewide, publicly funded program provides scholarships to students with disabilities to attend an eligible public or private school of their parents' choice. Students with either an Individualized Educational Program (IEP) or a Section 504 Plan are eligible for participation in the program. Students awarded scholarships are eligible to continue receiving them every year until they return to a public school, graduate from high school, or reach 22 years of age. Scholarships are awarded in the amount equal to the per-pupil expenditure in the traditional public school where the student is assigned or the amount of the private school's tuition and fees, whichever is the lesser amount. During the 2006–2007 academic year, McKay Scholarships ranged in amount from just over $5,000 to nearly $22,000, with an average award of about $7,000 (Winters & Greene, 2011). The number of students participating in the program has grown tremendously, in large part due to the great increase in the number of private schools willing to accept the voucher—from 100 schools in 2001 to 888 schools in 2009 (Winters & Greene, 2011). In 2012, the McKay Scholarship Program provided scholarships to over 20 thousand students.

Indiana

The Indiana Choice Scholarship Program (CSP) went into effect on July 1, 2011. Eligible students for the CSP include those whose family income does not exceed 150% of the amount required for eligibility in the federal-free and reduced-price lunch program. There is no requirement in Indiana that students live in a certain area, or currently attend a school designated as failing. Indiana's CSP is different from other voucher programs in a few ways. First, the scope of Indiana's program is much greater than most programs that have been enacted to date. Its eligibility requirements have drawn the ire of many traditional public school advocates as most children are eligible for participating in the program. Second, most voucher programs have been developed in response to either a perceived or real *crisis* situation for the state's or city's public education system. This is not the case in Indiana. In fact, public schools in Indiana have consistently been rated comfortably within the top 20 state education systems in the country.

But the CSP has been challenged on the grounds that it violates the Indiana state constitution's protection that taxpayers cannot be compelled to support religious institutions because the majority of schools that will receive funds through the program are sectarian schools. Article 1, Section 6 of the Indiana state constitution clearly prohibits the use of state funds to support any religious or theological institution. According to Eberle-Peay (2012), "Regardless of whether parents have a choice in sending their children to private schools, and whether that choice benefits those schools directly or indirectly, it is the taxpayers themselves who are compelled to support the sectarian schools" (p. 719).

Louisiana

After years of advocacy by school voucher proponents, in 2008, the Louisiana state legislature approved a $10 million voucher program for the city of New Orleans. The Student Scholarships for Educational Excellence Program provides for approximately 1,500 students attending persistently low-performing schools in New Orleans to receive tuition vouchers worth up to $6,300 to attend a secular or religious private school (Robelen & Cavanagh, 2008; Robelen, 2006). Students eligible for the program are those who (a) reside in the attendance area of a school district "found to be academically in crisis" pursuant to state statute; (b) have a family income not exceeding 250% of the federal poverty guidelines; and (c) are either entering kindergarten, or were enrolled in public school within a district in academic crisis with the school identified as academically unacceptable.

In 2012, the Louisiana state legislature passed a sweeping education reform bill that had significant implications for public and private school choices available to families in the state. First, and probably most notably, the new law instituted the largest statewide school voucher program in the country. Defending Louisiana governor Bobby Jindal's controversial education reform bill, Louisiana's superintendent of education John White said the governor's interest was not in creating a voucher school system for the state, but in creating "a system of choice and completion, one based on the decisions and needs of families" (Cavanagh, 2012, p. 15). Under this reform eligible children include those who attend a school that received a grade of C, D, or F on the state's school grading system and who live in a household with an annual income up to 250% of the poverty line (currently $57,625 for a family of four). Under the law more than half of the state's public school students would be eligible to receive state-funded scholarship that could be used to pay for tuition and fees at private and parochial schools across the state—including religious schools that integrate religious texts and references into the curriculum—and for individual courses offered by a menu of public and private providers including online options. Education policy professor Chris Lubienski called Louisiana's inclusion of funding provisions for individual course options a new dynamic in state education policy reflective of choice advocates' position that parents should have greater control over "the portion of the market they use" (Cavanagh, 2012, p. 17).

A group of plaintiffs, including most notably the Louisiana Federation of Teachers, brought suit against the Jindal administration on the grounds that the law was in violation of the Louisiana state constitution. And in December 2012, a Louisiana judge sided with the plaintiffs, declaring the funding mechanism for the state's highly contested new voucher program unconstitutional. The court ruled that Louisiana's school funding formula, the Minimum Foundation Program (MFP), was intended to be used exclusively for public schools. As expected, Louisiana governor Jindal and Louisiana State superintendent John White pledged to appeal the court's ruling and expressed optimism that on appeal the decision ould be reversed. But in reality, the court's ruling poses a big hurdle for school choice advocates in Louisiana to get past. While a much smaller voucher program in New Orleans had been paid for out of the state's general fund avoiding any potential issues with the MFP, the likelihood of funding such a large a statewide voucher program out of Louisiana's general fund is pretty slim.

Tax Credit Policies

State policies that grant education tax credits to individuals and/or corporations are a fast-growing part of the parent choice policy landscape. The idea of tax credit policies to provide aid to families sending their children to private schools is not new. The policy idea dates back at least to the 1960s when tax credit policies were proposed at both the federal and state levels, and even passed into law in some states. Most state tax credit policies were eventually ruled unconstitutional by courts that reasoned that such policies provided direct funding to religious institutions, an act prohibited by many state constitutions (Walch, 1984). Federal efforts during the 1980s to pass such policies went nowhere in Congress as they had no support from Congressional Democrats. However, federal tax credit policy for higher education tuition and expenses was supported by the Clinton administration. So in 1997 with the passage of the Taxpayer Relief Act of 1997, three college tuition tax credits were born: Hope Scholarships, Lifetime Learning Credits, and Education IRAs (individual retirement accounts) (Huerta & d'Etremont, 2007). Congressional Democrats supported the programs as they were limited to higher education and framed as measures to provide tax relief to families and expand access to higher education.

The recent popularity of tax credit policies, or NeoVouchers as termed by Welner (2008), may be attributed largely to tax credit policies being framed as an alternative to private school tuition vouchers. Additionally, as 37 states have some form of Blaine Amendment to their constitutions that prohibit the use of state funds to support sectarian organizations, tax credit policies may have significant legal advantages over voucher policies for those states (Huerta & d'Etremont, 2007). Tax credit policies may be politically framed as subsidies associated with tax policy, or as more universal and representing a direct return on individuals' tax efforts, avoiding being stigmatized, as vouchers have been, as a controversial education reform strategy (Huerta & d'Etremont, 2007). Further, because tax credits are funded from general state revenues, tax credits have not been as fiercely opposed as vouchers have been by traditional public school advocates (Huerta & d'Etremont, 2007). Arizona, Florida, and Pennsylvania are examples of states that have passed tax credit policies after having tried unsuccessfully to pass statewide voucher policies.

As with other choice policy measures, tax credit policies vary considerably by state, but the types of policies may be grossly divided into policies that provide tax credits to parents for educational expenses and policies that provide tax credits to corporations for donations. Policies directly benefiting parents in most states are not universal but are targeted to specific populations of students such as low-income students or students with special needs. Generally, parents benefit by receiving state income tax credits for expenses related to attending private schools. Policies benefiting corporations provide state corporate tax credits to business for donations made to nonprofit organizations, scholarship granting organizations (SGOs), that distribute scholarships to students to attend private schools. Legislation in most states with tax credit policies provide guidelines for what populations of students SGOs must provide scholarships to in order for corporations to receive tax credits for their donations. The following are just a few specific examples of current tax credit policies in the states.

Arizona

In 1997 Arizona passed a law allowing individuals to take a tax credit up to $500 for donations to organizations providing scholarships for students to attend private schools, and a tax credit up to $200 for donations to public school extracurricular activities (Kafer, 2009). Arizona's tax credit law has faced legal challenges. Plaintiffs, including the Arizona Education Association, Arizona School Boards Association, People for the American Way, and Americans United for Separation of Church and State, filed suit arguing that Arizona's tax credit law violated both the Establishment Clause of the US Constitution and the religious establishment provision of the Arizona Constitution. The Arizona Supreme Court upheld the law in 1999 holding that the law violated the provisions of neither the US Constitution nor the Arizona Constitution (Kafer, 2009).

Illinois

In 1999 the Illinois General Assembly passed an education tax credit law that gave families an annual credit up to 25% of education expenses that exceed $250, including tuition, up to a maximum of $500 per family. The Illinois law was also challenged in court by a teachers union. The Illinois Federation of Teachers challenged the law on the grounds that it violated the Illinois Constitution's religious establishment provisions. The law was upheld, however, in both the district and appellate courts.

Florida

Florida's corporate tax credit law, enacted in 2001, allows corporations to receive tax credits against their corporate income taxes for donations to approved scholarship organizations. Those corporate donations are then used to provide tuition scholarships to low-income students to attend an independent school or a voucher to attend a public school in another Florida school district. In 2012 approximately 38 thousand Florida students used these scholarships or vouchers to attend independent schools (Kafer, 2009).

Pennsylvania

Pennsylvania's tax credit program was enacted in 2001. Similar to Florida's corporate tax credit program, it allows corporations to receive a tax credit for either donations to scholarship programs or grants to public schools for innovative programs.

Parent Trigger Laws

Parent trigger laws have been enacted in 20 states across the US, including California, Texas, Louisiana, Connecticut, and Ohio. A parent trigger law has been discussed in education policy circles in North Carolina, but to date, no legislation has been introduced in the state general assembly. In general terms, variants of these laws give parents of children attending persistently failing schools the option of petitioning to change the schools' leadership and staff. In most cases, if a majority of parents of a given school sign such a petition, schools are forced to undergo significant re-staffing and/or reorganization. While the more popular choice policies such as charter schools and school vouchers give the parents the option to exit failing schools, parent trigger laws give parents the option to stay while insisting that schools undergo significant reform (Kelly, 2012). Parent trigger laws received a unanimous endorsement in 2012 from the US Conference of Mayors. Also, in 2012 the concept was popularized with the release of the motion picture *Won't Back Down*, which relays the story of a mother and a teacher who turn to a parent trigger law to try to force reform in their school.

As parent trigger laws are state-level reforms, the details of the policies vary considerably across states, but it is safe to say that these laws have triggered considerable controversies in most of the states where they exist, and few state's laws have drawn more controversy and national attention than California. In California, a majority of parents at a school that consistently fails to meet performance expectations can sign a petition and force the school into one of the federal government's four turnaround models: (a) converting of the school into a charter school; (b) replacing the principal and a minimum of half the school's staff, and giving the new principal greater control over personnel and budgeting decision-making; (c) replacing the principal and leaving the rest of the school's staff in place; or (c) closing the school down and redistributing the school's students to nearby higher-performing schools.

California's parent trigger law gained national attention when in 2010 a group of parents at an McKinley Elementary School in Compton invoked the law to have their school converted into a charter school the following year. A separate group of parents at McKinley, supported by the Compton Unified School District, organized in opposition to the conversion of McKinley alleging that the petitioners' actions had not been conducted in a public manner, and that they had been influenced by outside organizations. Parent Revolution, a Los Angeles-based parent choice advocacy group, had been actively organizing the parents of McKinley Elementary, educating them about the performance of the school, and had trained them in community organizing and leadership techniques. The California state school board asked the attorney general to investigate the parents complaints. As of 2012, the case was still tied up in litigation, but the petitioners were allowed to enroll their children in a charter school two blocks away from McKinley.

A few factors make parent trigger laws controversial. Proponents of such laws are optimistic that this new tool provided to parents whose children attend the most struggling schools will result in these schools being forced into major reforms, whereas previously, failing schools could continue to fail the children who attend them indefinitely. Critics of parent trigger laws, however, caution that "while mobilizing parents to overturn the status quo may be straightforward, encouraging stability and patience after the fact could be much more difficult" and "without sufficient attention to the rules and institutions necessary to build stability into the process, parent trigger laws may lead to the same policy churn, inefficiencies, and persistently troubled schools that exist today" (Kelly, 2012, p. 47). In other words, the same frustrations that led parents to sign petitions forcing schools into a reform model initially, could very well resurface just one year later, potentially threatening the very reforms that parents instituted the previous year. School reforms that do not produce quick turnarounds are especially susceptible to this trap, a process that has been referred to as *cycling* (Kelly, 2012) or *policy churn* (Hess, 1999). Adding to the controversy are teachers unions that have by and large opposed parent trigger laws, contending that there is no proof that the reforms triggered by parents lead to improved learning for children. It is also important to note, however, that some of the reform models that parents may choose using parent trigger laws could potentially weaken the power of teachers unions within schools and school districts.

Federal Choice Policy

The parent choice ideology was embodied by the federal *No Child Left Behind Act,* most notably through the accountability pressure applied by adequate yearly program (AYP) requirements. Under No Child Left Behind's (NCLB) opt out provision, parents of students attending schools that have consistently failed to meet AYP requirements have the option of attending a higher-performing school in the school district. This provision has drawn criticism from choice policy opponents who charge that the self-selection mechanism of any choice system results in the departure of students from "more academically oriented families with higher achieving students" (Mickelson & Southworth, 2005, p. 251). As a result, choice opponents caution, the struggling school loses funding, parental support, and "the student's contribution to the school's positive academic climate" (Mickelson & Southworth, 2005, p. 251).

The opportunity to transfer to a higher-performing school has not, however, resulted in droves of parents transferring out of persistently low-performing schools. While some degree of parents' not transferring their children to higher-performing schools can be explained as their choosing to remain in low-performing schools, much of it may also be explained by school districts employing tactics to reduce transfer numbers; tactics including delaying notification of parents of their right to transfer, failing to provide outreach to families eligible for transfers, and intentionally limiting available space at higher-performing district schools. Further, if most parents whose children were eligible to transfer to higher-performing schools chose to transfer, they would run out of school options pretty quickly since the number of children that qualify for transfers to a higher-performing school under NCLB's opt out provision greatly exceed the available placements for those students.

It was no secret that United States President George W. Bush supported the expansion of choice policies and school options for parents. Every year that he was in office President Bush's budget proposal included $75 million for a federal Choice Incentive Fund, which would have funded a five-city pilot school voucher project similar to the DC OSP. Those funding requests were never approved by Congress. Through NCLB, however, the administration was able to generously support the work of national choice advocacy organizations by providing them with a substantial boost from federal funding. Rod Paige, secretary of Education during the first term of the Bush administration, used the discretionary Fund for Innovation in Education to provide $77 million in funding to choice advocacy groups including BAEO, Hispanic CREO, the Center for Education Reform, and the Greater Educational Opportunities Foundation (DeBray-Pelot et al., 2007). Groups were to use those funds to educate parents about public school choice and supplemental education services options available to them under NCLB.

Most recently at the federal level, 2016 Republican presidential hopeful Senator Marco Rubio made a splash in the parent choice conversation by introducing legislation that would significantly expand choice. Rubio's proposed Educational Opportunities Act would create a federal corporate and individual tax credit for contributions to SGOs that provide scholarships to students for paying private school tuition and expenses. Rubio has characterized the proposed measure as part of an effort to create a twenty-first century middle class.

Final Thoughts

The parent choice policy landscape has become complex. Choice policies are complex. Choice reform models such as charter schools, vouchers, and tax credits have become common education policy jargon in our schools and our communities. Although more citizens have become aware of choice policy through the advocacy efforts of national and state organizations, including ones discussed in this chapter, very few people, educators included, truly understand how these policies work or the ideologies underlying them. The purpose of this chapter was to provide a general framework for the reader, including key definitions and examples of these policies at work in the states. In the following chapter I single out what has become the most popular choice reform model in the United States: charter schools. The popularity of the model does not mean that the politics surrounding charter schools has lessened. Charter school politics remains contentious in the nine states that have not yet adopted a charter school policy as well as in the states with current charter school legislation.

3

The Politics of Charter Schools

Charter schools are the fastest growing parent choice reform model in the United States. The charter school concept is attributed to a Massachusetts teacher, Ray Budde, who during the 1970s explored the idea of contracts for schooling in a similar vein to Henry Hudson's contract, or charter, with the East India Company to explore the Arctic in 1609. Budde estimated that a charter between teachers and parents could be similarly developed and used. Budde's charter school idea gained popularity with American Federation of Teachers (AFT) president Albert Shanker, who then pushed through the adoption of the charter school idea with the AFT (Bracey, 2002; Murphy & Shiffman, 2002).

Since Budde's initial idea, the charter school concept has expanded to include numerous arrangements and models, but the central idea of a contract or charter for providing educational services remains. The first actual charter school legislation was passed by the Minnesota legislature in 1991, and in 1993 Congress authorized $15 million for the Public Charter Schools Program as part of the Clinton administration's Improving America's Schools Act (Murphy & Shiffman, 2002). This funding supported a program of grants to states with charter school legislation. By 1995, 19 states had adopted charter school legislation. In 1998, Congress passed the Charter Schools Expansion Act, which increased federal funding of public charter schools from $15 million to $100 million for the 1999 fiscal year (Murphy & Shiffman, 2002). By 2000, 36 states had adopted charter school legislation. In May 2000, President Bill Clinton, with the goal of increasing the number of charter schools from 1,700 to 3,000, announced $16 million in new funding for charter schools and another $121 million in charter school continuation grants (Bracey, 2002). According to the National Alliance for Public Charter Schools and the Center for Education Reform, as of 2012, 41 states and the District of

Columbia had adopted some variant of charter school legislation, with roughly 6,600 charter schools in operation, serving over two million students. Recognized by both Harvard University and the Ford Foundation as one of the nation's best public policy initiatives (Nathan, 2002), charter schools have indeed become one of the most popular school reforms across the nation.

Charter school reform is a state-level education reform, so the idiosyncrasies of both individual charter schools and the state legislation that authorizes them make it difficult to speak about charter schools as a singular concept. For example, while Arizona's charter school law is based on the belief that market-like competition should bring about improvement in public schools and places no limits on the number of charter schools that can be authorized in the state or the number of students that can attend charter schools; Mississippi's law, through 2012, allowed only for the conversion of "chronically underperforming" schools into charters and permitted conversion of only 12 schools statewide with no more than three in a given year. To further complicate the issue, charter school reform means different things to different people. While free-market conservatives see charter schools as the first step toward an educational marketplace with full parental choice and competition between publicly and privately operated schools (Bulkley, 2005; Spring, 2005b); teachers unions, school board associations, and school and district level administrators who have supported charter school reforms see them as a means to improving the current public education setup (Bulkley, 2005; Stulberg, 2007); and cultural conservatives view charters as a way to increase parental control over values (Bulkley, 2005). Then some proponents of charter school reform have minimal interest in public education at all, and "see them as a means of making money" (Bracey, 2002, p. 65).

If anything is fundamental to charter schools it is that they are grounded in site-based management theory, which espouses that critical management decisions, including those concerning budget, human resources, curriculum, and pedagogy, should be made at the local school level, not the national, state, or even district central office levels (Cheng, 1996; Chubb & Moe, 1988; Nathan, 1996; Vergari, 2007). Thus, charter schools in most states are freed from some of the state and local regulation that traditional public schools are subject to, and charter school administrators enjoy considerably more discretion in school decision-making than their counterparts leading traditional public schools. For example, charter schools in North Carolina enjoy significant fiscal autonomy. The only restrictions on individual charter schools pertain to facilities spending. Charter schools may not use state funds to purchase real property or mobile classroom units. They may, however, use state funds to lease real property or mobile classroom units, and/or for payments on loans made to the school for facilities or equipment. With so few strings attached to charter school spending, charter school administrators in North Carolina have the choice of either spending school funds in a manner similar to traditional public schools or deviating from established patterns of school spending. North Carolina charter schools are subject to state financial audits and audit procedures and failure to meet state standards for fiscal management may result in the termination of a school's charter (Brown, 1999).

The greater degree of autonomy that charter schools enjoy is central to the charter school reform model. According to Chubb and Moe (1988), after taking into account family background, peer influences, and student aptitude, the most important determinant to promoting effective school organization is the degree of freedom from external control that a school enjoys; and an effectively organized school may be worth as much as an extra year's achievement over the course of a student's high school career. Generally speaking, traditional public schools have not enjoyed a great deal of decision-making authority at the local school level. Their management has been characterized as external control management, where "school management tasks are performed under instruction of the external central authority, often not in accordance with school characteristics and needs" (Cheng, 1996, p. 44). Traditional public school principals often have difficulty leading due to a mismatch between the degree of autonomy they believe that they need to be successful, and the amount of autonomy that they actually enjoy (Adamowski, Therriault, & Cavanna, 2007; Chubb & Moe, 1988).This is in contrast to private schools that on average enjoy significantly more autonomy in decision-making. Chubb and Moe (1988) note that given private schools' substantial autonomy, "it is not surprising to find that principals are stronger leaders; have greater control over hiring and firing; and that teachers are more integrally involved in policymaking" (p. 1085).

Greater autonomy for charter schools is provided in exchange for increased academic accountability, but accountability frameworks can vary considerably by state (Bracey, 2002; Bulkley, 2005; Hess, 2004). Whereas in some states charter schools are accountable to their authorizing boards, other states hold charter schools accountable to parents through the education marketplace, or through an amalgamation of performance-based, market-based, and bureaucratic accountability systems (Hassel & Vergari, 1999; Hess, 2004; Lewis & Fusarelli, 2010; Nathan, 1996; Shober, Manna, & Witte, 2006). This accountability for results principle is central to charter school reform across states (Anderson & Finnigan, 2001; Ascher et al., 2003). The accountability for results and site-based management tenets of charter school reform represent a fundamental shift in the way we think about public schooling (Fusarelli, 2001), forcing policy makers and school leaders alike to reconsider long-standing boundaries between what has been considered public and private.

Policy Monopolies, Charter Schools, and Change

A policy process framework is helpful in thinking about what the passage of charter school policies has represented in many states. Baumgartner and Jones's (1993) Punctuated Equilibrium Theory seems to be an appropriate choice for examining charter school policy. Punctuated equilibrium, now one of political sciences' leading models of policy change (McLendon & Cohen-Vogel, 2008), comes from evolution theory. In evolutionary biology, punctuated equilibrium represents an alternative to the Darwinian theory of evolution, which states that change occurs gradually over a long period of time. Punctuated equilibrium views evolutionary change as taking place "over long periods of stasis, in which species remain virtually unchanged, punctuated by relatively brief periods of intense change when new species are introduced, old ones die out, and existing ones undergo sudden transformations" (McLendon & Cohen-Vogel, 2008, p. 36).

Punctuated equilibrium theory's popularity in political science is largely attributable to the groundbreaking work of Baumgartner and Jones (McLendon & Cohen-Vogel, 2008). Baumgartner and Jones's (1993) development of punctuated equilibrium as a policy change theory grew out of their desire to explain policy change as more than just incremental adjustments over time. According to punctuated equilibrium theory, incrementalism is useful in describing policy change during certain periods, it does not account for periods of intense conflict and abrupt change. Baumgartner and Jones explain that "political processes are often driven by a logic of stability and incrementalism, but occasionally they also produce large-scale departures from the past" (True, Jones, & Baumgartner, 1999, p. 97). They argue that the United States' political system not only resists change through the complex institutions of separated powers and federalism, but also "provides numerous opportunities for policy entrepreneurs to try out new ideas" (Baumgartner & Jones, 1993, p. 100), just not at the same time and in the same place.

Periods of stability with incremental policy change come about as a result of a single interest having a monopoly over a policy issue. Baumgartner and Jones (1993) referred to this control as having a policy monopoly. They maintain that two essential characteristics define policy monopolies. First, a definable institutional structure is responsible for policy making and limiting access to the policy process. Second, a powerful supporting idea, which is generally connected to core political values and can be communicated through an image or rhetoric, is associated with the institution. Birkland (2005) observed that a policy monopoly has a keen interest in keeping policy making closed because closed systems benefit the interests of those in the monopoly. It follows then, that successful policy monopolies are able to influence the way that policy issues are defined and what images are associated with policy solutions (Baumgartner & Jones, 1993). Policy monopolies are able to "systematically dampen pressures for change" (p. 100), a process that Baumgartner and Jones refer to as negative feedback.

During periods of negative feedback "decision-making is decentralized to the iron triangles, and issue networks of specialists in the bureaucracy, congressional subgroups, and interested parties" (True et al., 1999, p. 102). Access to these subsystems is limited by two things: rules and norms that discourage the participation of outsiders and widespread positive understandings of the policy that stir up only support or indifference by those unaffected by the policy (Baumgartner & Jones, 1993). Thus, governmental institutional structures are often "rigged to favor subsystem participants and punish those who violate norms" (Lacireno-Paquet & Holyoke, 2007, p. 188). When citizens and policy actors on the outside of policy monopolies remain politically disengaged, policy is unlikely to change.

Policy monopolies, however, are not invulnerable. In the same way that they are constructed, they can and do collapse (True et al., 1999). Baumgartner and Jones (1993) asserted that interests on the outside of closed policy making subsystems may use the interaction between changing images and venues of public policy to break apart policy monopolies. By simultaneously changing the institutional place where policy decisions are made and forcing a redefinition of the policy issue, parties that were previously uninvolved are drawn into what becomes a debate on the macro-political stage as opposed to a closed policy subsystem. It is on this larger stage with increased attention that dramatic policy change will most often occur.

Baumgartner and Jones (1993) contended that "while concerned policymakers often strive toward the establishment of policy monopolies, such a state of affairs is remarkably difficult to sustain in the open American political system" (p. 8). There always lies the potential of shutout interests mounting an attack on seemingly impenetrable policy monopolies. According to Baumgartner and Jones, policy monopolies may completely break down or become more open issue networks, which have varying degrees of "mutual commitment or of dependence on others in the environment" (Heclo, 1995, p. 275).

Baumgartner and Jones (1993) define policy monopolies as stable policy subsystems that are able to both maintain control of images associated with their policies and restrict access to policy making. Even the most successful policy monopoly, however, are not invulnerable to penetration by outside interests. Conflict between policy monopolies and outside interests does occur. New interests that are able to successfully redefine policy issues, bringing conflict to the macro-political state, may topple policy monopolies and bring about new policy.

Punctuated equilibrium theory has been used by scholars examining educational policy change (Orr-Bement, 2002; Robinson, 2004; Sims & Miskel, 2003). Sims and Miskel applied punctuated equilibrium theory in explaining the rise of children's reading policy to the federal government agenda. They found that when broadly looking at reading policy, it did not appear that punctuation had occurred. In fact, they identified reading policy, in general, as a durable issue, one that had managed to remain on the federal government's agenda for a prolonged period of time. The changes that occurred with respect to the prominence of reading policy on the federal government's agenda were in reference to the target populations of the policy—children, adults, and so on. When looking at reading policy agenda status separated by the target populations of the policy, they found that it was children's reading policy entrepreneurs' ability to redefine problems that resulted in decisions about children's reading policy being taken out of closed policy subsystems and achieving prominence on the federal government's agenda in the 1990s. Similarly, in the current application of the theory, I consider the passage of charter school policies as policy punctuations in state education policy. Just as Sims and Miskel recognized the role of reading policy entrepreneurs in redefining and reframing reading policy issues, I recognize the roles that charter school policy entrepreneurs have played in redefining problems about public education and effectively penetrating seeming impenetrable state education policy subsystems to bring about major change in state public education policy, and arguably, a reconceptualization of public schooling in their states. Taken collectively, these changes have arguably resulted in a reconsideration of the nature of public schooling in America.

Lacireno-Paquet and Holyoke (2007) raise the question of whether new policies, such as the passage of charter school legislation, are enduring or short-lived. They argue that long-held issue definitions do not suddenly melt away, and "once powerful but now displaced legislators and lobbyists meekly accept their defeat and fade into the night" (p. 190). Rather, displaced interests fight to reassert the original status quo, possibly shopping for more favorable venues to move the fight to, or engaging in grassroots strategies and other forms of outside advocacy. Instead of a punctuation being a clean victory for new interests, they assert that it may only be "the opening shots in an advocacy war, as long-standing definitions and structures are toppled but new ones have not yet clearly emerged and taken root as a new enduring and stable subsystem" (p. 191). They further emphasize that it is only when once powerful interests are unable to reassert themselves that a new status quo may become embedded and last for a considerable amount of time (until the next punctuation).

Fierce opposition by displaced interests in several states to the expansion of charter schools in number, enrollment, and autonomy supports Lacireno-Paquet and Holyoke's (2007) hypothesis. According to Williams (2007), some opponents of charter school expansion have waged war at the state level by lobbying against legislation that would expand charter school reform, and at the local level by making it difficult for charter schools to receive authorization from local school boards or secure buildings and land for schools. Perhaps the most significant accomplishment of displaced interests across the states has been their preventing the removal of caps on the number of charter schools that may be authorized in a state. About 20 states have some type of limit on the number of charters schools that may be authorized (National Alliance for Public Charter Schools, 2008). Maintaining caps on the number of charter schools authorized in states has effectively constrained charter school growth (Ziebarth, 2007).

Displaced interests have also attacked the positive policy images that choice advocates have associated with charter schools. Although charter schools continue to grow in number and popularity, there has been a proliferation of research showing no significant advantages of children attending charter schools, and in some cases negative effects for charter school students (Barr, Sadovnik, & Vosconti, 2006; Robelen, 2006; Sass, 2006; Zimmer & Buddin, 2007). A reanalysis of fourth grade National Assessment for Educational Progress (NAEP) test score data, for example, showed that traditional public school students outperformed charter school students in both mathematics and reading (Robelen, 2006). The long-term political effects of this research are still unfolding.

Interest Group Politics

The politics of education has been said to be largely the politics of interest groups (Fusarelli, 2008; Mawhinney, 2001; Spring, 2005a). Interest groups can be broadly defined as "voluntary associations organized to pursue a common interest (or interests) through political participation, toward the ultimate goal of getting favorable public policy decisions from government" (Spitzer, Ginsberg, Lowi, & Weir, 2002, p. 7). Interest groups with varying degrees of influence over public policy have formed all across the United States. A few widely recognized examples of interest groups include the National Rifle Association, the National Restaurant Association, the American Humane Association, the Sierra Club, and the National Organization for Women. Prominent national education interest groups include the American Federation of Teachers, the National Education Association, the National School Boards Association, and the National Association of Elementary School principals. According to pluralist theory, more than these groups serving as vehicles for certain factions to achieve their own relatively narrow aims, interest group politics may serve as a vital link between citizens and governments (Spitzer et al., 2002; Van Horn, Baumer, & Gormley, 1989).

A basic understanding of pluralism is essential for understanding the politics of interest groups and interest group behavior at any level. Based on theories of American democracy developed during the 1950s and 1960s, pluralist theory states that competition among interests will result in balance, with all the interests regulating each other and each group likely having to accommodate some of the policy desires of other groups in order to achieve its own aims (Birkland, 2005; Fowler, 2004; Gupta, 2001; Spitzer et al., 2002).

However, even the broad array of interest groups in the United States does not represent all interests equally. Neither may we be assured that competition between interest groups will result in public policies that codify the *common good* (Spitzer et al., 2002). Indeed, the most serious and most frequent critique leveled against pluralist theory is that it is biased in favor of those with money and power; or as Schnattschneider (1960) put it, "The flaw in the pluralist heaven is that the heavenly chorus sings with a strong upper-class accent" (p. 35). We cannot be sure that all interests are represented proportionally, and that this competition among interests will result in what is best for the public. Additionally, the issue of who has the ability to participate in interest group politics arises. Spitzer et al. (2002) observe that "well educated, upper-income business and professional people are more likely to have the time and money and to have acquired through the educational process the concerns and skills needed to play a role in a group or association" (p. 199).

Nevertheless, interest groups are undeniably key actors in the public policy process (Birkland, 2005; Spitzer et al., 2002), and there are many different types of interests that are represented by groups. Some of these interest groups include professional associations such as the American

Bar Association and the National Education Association (NEA), public interest groups such as the National Resources Defense Council, ideological groups such as the Christian Coalition, and public sector groups such as the North Carolina School Boards Association and the National League of Cities (Spitzer et al., 2002; Van Horn et al., 1989). The number of interest groups in the United States has grown exponentially in recent years (Baumgartner & Leech, 2001; Mawhinney, 2001; Spitzer et al., 2002), and the diversity of these groups in terms of size, resources, leadership, cohesiveness, and prestige varies greatly (Fusarelli, 2008; Opfer et al., 2008, Spitzer et al., 2002; Van Horn et al., 1989).

The relatively recent explosion of interest group activity has led some scholars to believe that the influence of any one interest group acting alone has been considerably diminished (Baumgartner & Jones, 1993; Salisbury, 1990). Hojnacki (1997), for instance, contends that "to be effective, rational group leaders must choose strategies that enhance their chances for advocacy success" (p. 62). As a result, scholars have documented a proliferation of interest group coalitions both within and across policy domains, hoping to wield greater power and influence than they would wield working as individual groups (Hula, 1995; Opfer et al., 2008; Sabatier & Jenkins-Smith, 1999). This is not to suggest, however, that all interest groups must operate as members of coalitions. Hojnacki (1997) found that interest groups weigh the costs and benefits of joining alliances before making these decisions. She states:

> Specifically, when a group's interest in an issue is narrow, and when a group's potential allies signal that they have little to contribute to a collective advocacy campaign, the cost of joining an alliance will likely outweigh any benefits that may accrue. But when organization perceived to be pivotal to success are members of an alliance, and when groups represent expressive interests or perceive a strong organized opposition, the benefits of coalition are substantial. (p. 62)

Thus, the decision appears to be a strategic one. Interest groups do not blindly join alliances. Rather, they do so when they believe that there is something to gain from it.

Education Interest Groups

Education interest groups share many of the characteristics of interest groups broadly. Opfer (2001) reported that in 1999 there were 650 individual education interest groups (Opfer, 2001), most of which could be divided into what Spring (2005a) called the big three: the corporate sector, foundations, and teachers' unions. Generally speaking, education interest groups have been active in state education policy-making arenas. In an analysis of 20 case studies of state decision-making on education issues from 1971 to 1991, Mazzoni (1993) found that education interest groups had long had a voice in state education policy. In Minnesota, these groups included the state's two teachers unions, the Minnesota School Boards Association, and various *outside groups* including a Twin Cities public interest group, the Citizens League, and a big business lobbying organization, the Minnesota Business Partnership (Mazzoni, 1993). Education interest group presence, however, has not always resulted in interest groups having significant influence over policy. In an analysis of school reform activity across all 50 states during the mid-1980s, Feir (1995) found that "traditional education interest groups, even in those states in which such groups tend to be relatively strong, played minor roles in the 1983–1987 education reform" (p. 28).

The coalition behavior of education interest groups has also been documented in the scholarly literature, with particular emphasis on coalition activity in school choice politics (DeBray-Pelot et al., 2007; Kirst, 2007; Fusarelli, 2003; Opfer et al., 2008; Vergari, 2007). Some might find the relatively large number of education interest groups and coalitions as surprising given that some interest group scholars have concluded that when groups produce public or collective goods, such as education, members tend to lose the incentive to participate in group activities because they will receive the benefits whether they are members or not (Olson, 1965; Opfer, 2001). Olson's (1965) rational choice model, which referred to this as the free rider problem, "assumes that individuals are rational decision makers who wish to maximize the benefits accruing from the use of their time and money to participate in groups by ensuring that those benefits are greater than the costs of participation" (Mawhinney, 2001, p. 194). However, Opfer (2001) argued that rational choice theories of interest group maintenance assuming self-interest cannot explain the perseverance of education interest groups, and that a theory accounting for levels of ideological commitment is more appropriate for explaining the maintenance and commitment of these groups.

I, however, argue that education interest groups tend not to suffer from the free rider problem because most groups are not lobbying for public goods. A closer examination of education or education-related interest groups reveals that their interests are typically much narrower than improvement of education, and the goods they fight for are typically enjoyed primarily by members of the interest group and not by the public at large. For example, the NEA, while an education interest group, exists to represent and fight for the interests of its members, teachers.

The NEA does not exist for the purpose of protecting or fighting for the best of interest of children or the public. I am not suggesting that the NEA does not want what is in the best interest of children. I contend that the group exists first and foremost for the purpose of protecting the interests of teachers, and it fights for children's educational rights only to the extent that that goal converges with protecting the interests of teachers. For example, when an NEA or AFT affiliate chapter stages a teacher strike, it does so not because its local school district resists providing children with educational services; instead, it stages a strike because the local school district has failed to meets its demands that typically involve teacher salaries, benefits, and evaluations.

Consider also the National School Boards Association (NSBA), which while likely is very interested in policies that are supportive of public education, also undeniably acts self-interestedly. The organization states very clearly on its website that it "represents the interests of the nation's 90,000 local school board members in Congress." Please note that the organization does not explicitly state that it represents the interests of the children served by the nation's local school boards. NSBA has been quite clear about its policy position on charter schools. In its January 2013 Issue Brief, NSBA asserts its conditional support of charter schools, with the conditions being that charter schools are authorized only by the local school boards in the communities where charter schools are to be located, and with local school boards making decisions about new charter school applications, charter school accountability, and the renewal of charters. As of 2013, local school boards served as authorizers for over half of all charter schools in the United States, and the NSBA policy brief shows that it has every intention on expanding local boards' authority over charter schools.

So would NSBA's policy position on charter schools be one that is legitimately and solely after ensuring that high-quality educational services are provided to children? It is not. School boards want to maintain control over the public educational services offered in their communities. School boards see charter schools operating in their communities outside of the auspices of the local school board as competition to traditional public schools. They see these schools as a threat, attracting students and the local, state, and federal funds that follow them away from traditional public schools and into the coffers of charter schools. I would not go nearly so far as to suggest that the organization's motives are malicious, but I do contend that its motives are self-interested, and achieving its policy goals would be first and foremost in the interest of its dues-paying members, school boards. I am not suggesting that NSBA and teachers unions are the only self-interested education and education-related interest groups, instead my argument is that most of these groups act self-interestedly. Whether it be the American Library Association, the National Parent Teacher Association, or the National Association of Elementary School Principals, these groups act politically to ensure that the interests of its membership are protected. Its members recognize that benefit and gladly join the organizations, not because the organizations fight for what is best for children, but because the organizations fight to protect the interests of their members.

I further contend that Olsen's free rider problem may not apply to education and education-related interest groups because even if groups were truly lobbying for public education, public education is not a purely public good. I made the argument in chapter 1 that public education is most accurately described as a hybrid good—both public good and private good all at the same time. While society writ large clearly benefits from the provision of public educational services, the direct recipients of those services benefits considerably. Consider the child whose public education enables her to go on to college and medical school and become a neurosurgeon. Society will clearly benefit from her contributions to health and medicine, but she and her family will benefit considerably as well through her medical career made possible in large part by high-quality public education.

Interest Group Strategies

Interest group strategies can be divided into five categories: electoral politics, lobbying, going public, access, and litigation (Austen-Smith, 1993; Spitzer et al., 2002). Interest groups attempt to influence electoral politics by either funding candidates for political office or direct campaign activism (Spitzer et al., 2002; Van Horn et al., 1989). Many interest groups that fund political candidates do so through political action committees (PACs). PACs are created when interest groups get involved with electoral politics. These committees raise and distribute funds to political candidates on behalf of interest groups. Education and education-related PACs can play a significant role in electoral politics at the local, state, and national levels. The NEA (not including its state-level subsidiaries) made political contributions through PACs from 2000 to 2012 in the amount of over $53,000,000 with about 7% going to Democratic candidates (including $8,000 to NC Governor Bev Perdue in 2008), less than 1% going to Republicans, and over 93% of contributions going to support or defeat ballot measures. Interestingly, from 2002 to 2012 the NEA donated over $1,000,000 to the North Carolina Democratic Party, including $100,000 in 2012 and over $300,000 in 2008. The NEA's PAC contributions to the North Carolina Democratic Party were more than double what it donated to any other state party during that time period.

Between 2003 and 2012 the North Carolina Association of Educators (NCAE) made PAC contributions totaling $898, 202. Democrats received nearly 95% of NCAE's PAC contributions, Republicans received just over 5% of contributions, and less than 0.5% of contributions went toward supporting or defeating ballot measures. NCAE's top contributions' recipients included Senate Education Committee member Sen. Martin Nesbit (D) who received almost $23,000; former speaker of the House Rep. Joe Hackney (D) who received $17,000; former president *pro tempore* of the Senate Sen. Marc Basnight (D) who received over $16,000; former senator, lieutenant governor, and gubernatorial candidate Walter Dalton (D) who received over $16,000; and former lieutenant governor and governor Bev Perdue (D) who received $11,000.

NEA subsidiaries have active PACs that play significant roles in state electoral politics not only in NC, but all across the United States. For example, the Kentucky Education Association (KEA) made contributions totaling $722,898 from 2003 to 2012. Democrats received nearly 72% of KEA's contributions, Republicans received about 27% of contributions, and about 1.5% of contributions went toward supporting or defeating ballot measures. One notable recipient of KEA's PAC contributions has been chair of the House Education Committee, Rep. Carl Rollins (D). Rollins has received a total of $6,000 in contributions from KEA's PAC from 2006 to 2012, including $1,000 in 2006, $2,000 in 2010, and $2,000 in 2012. At the local level in Kentucky, from 2003 to 2012 the Jefferson County Teachers Association (JCTA) has made PAC contributions totaling over $112,000, with about 85% of contributions going to Democratic candidates, about 11% going to Republican candidates, and just over 4% going to nonpartisan candidates (typically local school board candidates). From 2003 to 2012, JCTA donated $13,500 to the Kentucky Democratic Party, $1,000 to the Kentucky Senate Democratic Caucus, and $500 to the Kentucky Republican Party.

Most interest groups that sponsor PACs, in addition to making contributions, also maintain active lobbying operations; "as a result, campaign contributions and lobbying often occur together" (Wright, 1990, p. 418). For example, both the NEA and the AFT promote the interests of their members through a combination of supporting political candidates and lobbying government officials at the local, state, and federal levels (Spring, 2005a). State and local interest group subsidiaries including NCAE, KEA, and JCTA coordinate contributions and lobbying efforts as well.

In addition to PAC contributions and lobbying, interest groups may use the strategy of *going public*. Going public can be defined as an effort to "mobilize the widest and most favorable climate of opinion," and may include advertising, boycotts, strikes, rallies, marches, and sit-ins (Spitzer et al., 2002). This strategy of mobilizing an issue's constituency was used effectively by an interest group alliance in Minnesota in an effort to mobilize citizens in support of tax concessions for private school parents (Mazzoni & Malen, 1985). The groups that formed this alliance did not enjoy institutional access. Access refers to interest groups' involvement in the decision-making process. Spitzer et al. (2002) observes that "access is usually a result of time and effort spent cultivating a position within the inner councils of government" (p. 205). Not having this advantage, the Minnesota alliance resorted to going public, or what Schnattschneider (1960) called expanding the scope of conflict. According to Mazzoni and Malen (1985):

> The alliance mobilized external resources to influence the policy-making process.... The constraints imposed or threatened by an issue constituency were the main source of that alliance's power to establish priority for its issue on the legislative agenda, prevent favorable bills from being blocked in the decision-making process, and obtain majority committee and floor votes. (p. 111)

Similarly, Feir (1995) showed that even in states where traditional education interest groups tend to be relatively strong, expanding the scope of conflict over education reform to include business and political leaders and the media can result in traditional education interest groups being denied the privileges of establishing the agenda and significantly influencing policy.

Finally, interest groups may use litigation strategies to influence policy. These strategies include filing suit against government agencies, financing suits against the government brought by individuals, or filing briefs as amicus curiae to existing cases (Austen-Smith, 1993; Spitzer et al., 2002). Manno, Finn, & Vanourek (2000a) argued that interest groups engage in litigation strategies as a way to slow or completely prevent school choice legislation. In fact, in Michigan, groups opposing school vouchers successfully used state courts to halt the passage of school voucher legislation (Bulkley, 2005; Mintrom, 2002).

Whatever strategies an interest group chooses to pursue, its objective is to persuade policy makers and influence legislation in a way that is favorable to its members. The degree of influence that interest groups actually have, however, is extremely variable. While some interest groups are able to exercise considerable influence over policy decision, others have little to no influence at all (Opfer et al., 2008). Research suggests that having substantial amounts of money, committed members, strong leadership, and a favorable reputation all contribute to interest groups being able to influence public policy (Spitzer et al., 2002; Van Horn et al., 1989). Opfer et al. (2008) offered that

> interest groups will have a high probability of affecting policy outcomes when they face little or no opposition from other policy actors or policy actors are undecided on an issue. Interest groups are also likely to be successful at influencing policy outcomes when an issue is highly technical or complex, nonpartisan and nonideological, or receives little public or media attention. (p. 200)

At the federal level, Wright (1990) found in an analysis of the voting decisions within the US House of Representatives ways and means that campaign contributions were significant in helping groups to gain access, but not to the extent that they secured representatives' votes. Wright (1990) commented:

> Representatives' voting decisions in committee, particularly in the Ways and Means Committee, are best explained here by the number of lobbying contacts they received from groups on each side of the issue. Campaign contributions proved to be useful predictors of groups' lobbying patterns; but once lobbying was controlled, little evidence was found in support of a direct link between money and voting. (p. 433)

Also, Wright noted that groups that chose to distribute their contributions broadly across party and ideological spectrums gained considerable flexibility in terms of who they were able to subsequently lobby, getting an advantage over groups that chose to only distribute contributions to their partisan and ideological friends.

Austen-Smith (1993) suggested that interest groups' ability to influence legislators may occur only through changing beliefs; "and the extent to which any information offered to alter beliefs is effective depends on the credibility of the lobbyist to the legislator in question" (p. 800). According to Austen-Smith (1993):

> Such credibility...depends partly upon how closely the lobbyist's preferences over consequences reflect those of the legislator being lobbied, and on how confident is the legislator being lobbied, and on how confident is the legislator that the lobbyist is in fact informed. (p. 800)

The stage of the policy process in which an interest group chooses to lobby may also have effects on its influence. For example, groups must identify stages at which they should lobby: the full legislature at the agenda-setting stage, the committee at the committee stage, the full legislature at the voting stage, or at all stages. Austen-Smith (1993) argued that both the character of the information transmitted, as well as the nature of the influence exerted is likely to differ between stages of the policy process.

> First, there exist circumstances under which influential lobbying can take place at both stages of the process, but the structure of the information offered at each stage is distinct; second, that agenda stage lobbying can be influential even when the House's most preferred policy consequence lies between those of the committee and those of the lobbyist; and third, that more information can be offered here, where it is occasionally uncertain whether the lobbyist is informed or not, than is possible in environments where the committee is known to possess information surely. (p. 801)

Interest group strategies may be dependent on a range of factors including context, the nature of the issue, the degree of conflict involved, the public salience of the issue, the strategies of other groups, and the orientation taken by the decision makers (Baumgartner & Leech, 1996; Mawhinney, 2001). For example, in examining the political strategies of national educational interest groups, Opfer (2001) found that changes in legislative turnover that denied once-privileged interest groups access to government decision-making did not result in these groups merely folding up and moving on. Rather, she found that these groups resorted to "nonaccess requiring" techniques, including letter writing, contributing to political campaigns, and grassroots mobilization. Opfer's findings support those of Gais and Walker's (1991), who found that interest groups that do not enjoy government access resort to tactics such as protest, and other forms of grassroots lobbying and mobilization.

Venue

A key tactical decision that interest groups must make is with respect to venue. Federalism, separation of powers, and jurisdictional overlaps serve the dual purposes in punctuated equilibrium theory of inhibiting change during periods of negative feedback and providing opponents of stable policy subsystems with multiple venues to seek a foothold in the policy process during periods of positive feedback (True et al., 1999). Multiple venues in the American political system constitute "multiple opportunities for policy entrepreneurs to advance their case" (True et al., 1999, p. 101). Similarly, Van Horn et al. (1989) noted that "the fragmented, decentralized policy system is highly permeable to groups outside of government"

(p. 15). Choosing a venue need not be a one or the other type decision. "Policy venues may be monopolistic or shared, that is, a single issue may simultaneously be subject to the jurisdiction of several institutions, or it may be within the domain only of one set of institutions" (Baumgartner & Jones, 1993, p. 31). As such, interest groups seeking change in public policy may shop for the best venue or venues in which to press their claims (Baumgartner & Jones, 1993; Birkland, 2005).

Possible venues or points of access for interest groups include legislatures, legislative committees and subcommittees, government executives, administrative agencies, and the courts—most of these being available options at the federal, state, and local levels (Baumgartner & Jones, 1993; Birkland, 2005; Fowler, 2004; Kingdon, 2003; True et al., 1999). The media is also a venue that may be available to interest groups. Cooper, Fusarelli, and Randall (2004) assert that the media plays a critical role in determining how quickly policy issues' rise to prominence on government agendas. Additionally, the media has the effect of influencing both the general public and policy makers to think more about some issues and less about others. According to Birkland (2005), groups and policy makers use the media as trial balloons:

> Strategic leaks of information [to the media] are common, particularly when policy makers are preparing large and complex policy initiatives. From public reaction to these trial balloons, policy makers can make adjustments to their proposals or learn whether they are likely to succeed or fail. (p. 212)

Interest group activity in the courts is less visible than other venues (Spitzer et al., 2002; Van Horn et al., 1989). The courts, however, have been instrumental in interest groups gaining a foothold in the policy process when legislatures and administrative agencies have been less receptive. Interest groups may employ several strategies in the courts. They may use funds to back legal cases that have some policy significance, and may even play a hand in judge selection by lobbying executives and legislators on behalf of court nominees, or attempting to influence election contests for the bench (Van Horn et al., 1989).

Interest groups' choices about lobbying in one venue as opposed to another may be impacted by the lobbying decisions of both allied and opposing groups. Holyoke (2003) found that interest groups choose to avoid venues where opposing groups have a great deal of influence. Holyoke asserted:

> Interest groups may concentrate their efforts in a venue, or venues, where the array of players is more sympathetic. In unfriendly venues, interest

groups may engage in pro-forma lobbying, reserving their greatest efforts for venues in which the cards are not stacked against them. (p. 335)

Holyoke's findings are in agreement with what other research on interest group strategies has shown: that interest group decisions, in general, are impacted a great deal by "what groups know about other organizations active in a policy area and the actions taken by these organizations" (Hojnacki, 1997, p. 62).

Problem Definition

Education and education-related interest groups are often ones that can successfully define issues as problems that favor their intended course of action, or redefine problems in such a manner that the interest group's intended course of action becomes for the public at least plausible, but optimally, seen as the best course of action to take. All societal conditions do not come to be defined as problems (Birkland, 2005; Fowler, 2004; Kingdon, 2003; Rochefort & Cobb, 1994; Stone, 2002). Fowler (2004) notes that "we put up with all manner of conditions every day: bad weather, unavoidable and untreatable illnesses, pestilence, poverty, fanatacism" (p. 109). These conditions only become defined as problems once society comes to believe that government should, and is able to, do something about them (Fowler, 2004; Kingdon, 2003; Rochefort & Cobb, 1994). Kingdon (2003) further assesses that problems are not simply the conditions or external events themselves, rather "there is also a perceptual, interpretive element" (p. 109). To further illustrate this point Kingdon quotes an employee of the Department of Health, Education, and Welfare:

> We live with these social problems for a while, and then we finally decide that if we're serious about them we should do it. The problem doesn't have to get any worse or any better. It doesn't have to be some major change in the problem. Take poverty. Poverty didn't get any worse. Lyndon Johnson just decided to undertake this war on poverty. Why one moment seems better than another I don't know. (p. 110)

Similarly, Birkland (2005) observed that prior to the development of the polio vaccine, this illness was seen as only a condition that perhaps could be avoided. After the development of the vaccine, however, polio came to be regarded as a problem about which something could be done. In the particular case of polio, it became a problem about which government could do something. "Conditions become defined as problems when policymakers have the technical ability and political will to address them" (Cooper et al., 2004, p. 65).

Problem definition is the process by which societal conditions are transformed into public problems (Kingdon, 2003). Put differently, "it is an assertion that particular conditions, such as student test scores, fail to meet acceptable standards.... Different standards of judgment, different explanations of causation, and different solutions can be used to define the same problem" (Portz, 1996, p. 372). It is a "recursive process of debate and persuasion among policy actors with different values, preferences, and resources, and it involves a multifunctional purpose in political discourse" (Young, Lewis, Tate, Grant, & Thomas, 2008, p. 2). The process is recursive in that it may be repeated indefinitely. Problems may be continually redefined. According to Mazzoni and Malen (1985), "Issues are redefined to enhance their attractiveness; redefinitions raise policy conflicts from specific contexts to general concerns, from referential to condensational symbols" (p. 112). How a problem is defined or redefined is integral to the nature of political debate, the level of conflict, public and interest group participation, and the consideration of policy solutions (Cooper et al., 2004, Young et al., 2008). Thus, "problem definition is strategic because groups, individuals, and government agencies deliberately and consciously fashion portrayals so as to promote their favored course of action" (Stone, 2002, p. 133). Problem definition is equally as important to determining what policies do not make it to the governmental agenda, as determining which ones do (Cooper et al., 2004; Stone, 2002). Spring (2005a) writes of ways that different interests could potentially spin a newspaper headline reading, "Lower Test Scores in City Schools":

> A religious right group might give a spin that lower scores exemplify the lack of instruction in traditional moral values. Another group might spin an interpretation that lower scores are the result of low academic standards. A spokesperson for a teachers' union might put the following spin on the story: low teacher salaries make it impossible to keep good teachers, causing test scores to fall. (p. 63)

Fowler (2004) insisted that "developing an attractive image of the issue and associating appealing symbols with it in order to attract public attention" are integral to the process problem definition. A policy's image refers to how a policy is understood and discussed (Baumgartner & Jones, 1993). These images are critical in determining whether issues are expanded to groups that were previously apathetic (Baumgartner & Jones, 1993). Changes in policy image are essential to breaking apart policy monopolies and changing the policies that they protect. To put it simply, new images attract new participants (True et al., 1999).

Birkland (2005) noted that increased attention to a problem usually means greater negative attention, thus leading to changes in images associated with policies. Baumgartner and Jones (1993) cited the breakdown of the 1970s nuclear power monopoly as an example of changing policy image. The once stable nuclear policy monopoly consisted of the Atomic Energy Commission (AEC), the nuclear utilities, builders of nuclear power plants, the civilian and military nuclear establishment, and the Joint Committee on Atomic Energy (JCAE). Interest groups, the media, and eventually the public voiced increasing concern over the safety and cost of nuclear power, resulting in the collapse of this once-stable policy monopoly. The JCAE was disbanded, the AEC broke up, and the Nuclear Regulatory Commission was created. "The increased scrutiny of the industry began to break down the image of nuclear power as 'the peaceful atom' creating power 'too cheap to meter' to an image of danger and expense" (Birkland, 2005, p. 229).

Stone (2002) posited that policy actors' use of language, particularly in the development of causal stories, is also a critical component of problem definition. Causal stories are narrative descriptions of the causes of problems that often include normative statements both about the particular problem as well as whom or what is responsible for the problem. Symbols, numbers, causes, interests, and decisions, she argued, are all tools that policy actors use to craft these stories. Stone differentiates between different types of causal stories, stating that

> intentional causal stories are strong because they outrage people; they suggest conspiracy or willful malevolence. Accidental causal stories are strong because they checkmate policy activists; after all, if a problem is caused by accidents of fate or nature, no human intervention can prevent it (though policies can alleviate some of its consequences). The other two types of stories are relatively weak (mechanical cause and inadvertent cause), because they don't pin much moral responsibility on anyone. If you want to make a persuasive argument in a political controversy, use a strong causal story. (pp. 401–402)

Portz (1996) sought to determine why some problem definitions achieve prominence on the education policy agenda in Boston, while others do not. His findings revealed that problem definition was central to guiding policy deliberations and responses to concerns in the Boston Public Schools. Portz concluded that there was bias in the policy process, whereby "problem definitions that are more visible, adopted by powerful political sponsors, and attached to viable solutions stand a better chance of receiving recognition and action on the policy agenda" (p. 382). In essence, how a problem comes to be defined and understood, is a function of not only the substance of the argument, but also who presents the argument, and who hears the argument.

Focusing Events

External events can disrupt stable subsystems and help to reinforce policy images (Baumgartner & Jones, 1993, Birkland, 2005; Fowler, 2004; John, 2003; True et al., 1999). Birkland (2005) referred to these events as focusing events, and contended that these events give groups the opportunity to attract a great deal of attention to an issue and press for change. In Baumgartner and Jones's (1993) example of the breakdown of the nuclear power monopoly, both the accident at the Three Mile Island nuclear plant in Pennsylvania in 1979 and the default on bonds sold to build nuclear power plants in Washington State in 1982 served to reinforce the negative policy images of nuclear power being dangerous and expensive. Birkland (2005) cited other examples of focusing events that had the effect of reinforcing policy images, including the Rodney King beating, the beatings of African Americans during civil rights marches in the 1960s, and the 1963 march on Washington. While these disruptions are rarely enough alone to change a policy image, they may be particularly useful in reinforcing policy images or perceptions, and focusing attention on problems that may have already been "in the back of people's minds" (Kingdon, 2003, p. 98).

Also noteworthy is the idea that focusing events may at times have the effect of not only reinforcing policy images, but also making venues available to groups that were not available before. For example, prior to the Exxon Valdez oil spill, environmentalists groups were quite limited in the venues available to them to draw attention to the threat of an oil spill in Prince William Sound. Following the oil spill, however, "fishing and environmental interests had new venues in which to press their claims, particularly in the news media and in congressional hearings, whereas before the spill these hearings were dominated by industry interests" (Birkland, 2005, p. 101).

Charter School Politics

Charter School Policy Adoption

Scholarship attempting to explain why and when states adopt charter school legislation may be organized into three categories: studies that explore internal state determinants, studies that explore interstate relational factors, and studies that consider both. Looking at intrastate factors, Wong and Shen (2002) tested the relationship between state adoption of charter school legislation and a set of state-specific political variables including political party dominance, amount of political competition, and state climate toward private schools. They found an inverse relationship between the average rate of high school completion and a state's likelihood of adopting charter school legislation. Using a multivariate event history analysis model, Wong and Langevin (2007) tested the relationship between state's decisions to adopt charter school legislation and a set of independent variables including political and economic influences, social influences, and geographic influences. Their results indicated that state adoption was significantly related to partisan gubernatorial control, classroom spending, private schools, education finance litigation, and minority representation. Geographic influence variable were not significantly related to state adoption.

Renzuli and Roscigno (2005), however, did find a significant relationship between state adoption of charter school legislation geographic influences. Specifically, they found that states were more likely to adopt charter school legislation if they had regional states with strong charter school laws. The difference in findings may be attributed to how they measured the geographical region variable. Whereas Renzuli and Roscigno considered the strength of the charter school laws of neighboring states, Wong and Langevin (2007) considered only whether nearby states had adopted any form of charter school policy. Despite differences, both Renzulli and Roscigno, and Wong and Langevin suggest that both internal and interstate factors may be significant in explaining the adoption of charter school legislation.

Stoddard and Corcoran (2006) studied the circumstances under which states were likely to pass laws favorable to charter schools, and under which conditions charter school participation was likely to be high. They found that demographics, teacher union participation, and student performance were all statistically significant determinants of state charter school legislation adoption and charter school participation. Also, controlling for student performance, states with higher Hispanic populations were more likely to adopt charter school legislation, and more likely that the legislation would be favorable to charter schools. In contrast, states with higher Black populations were not more likely to adopt charter school legislation, but those states with charter schools did have higher rates of charter school participation. States with higher SAT scores were also found to be less likely to pass charter school legislation. However, no significant relationship between SAT scores and charter school participation were found. Finally, the results indicated that states with higher percentages of teachers covered by a union contract were less likely to pass charter school legislation in the 1990s, and if they passed charter school legislation at all, it was more likely to be restrictive to charter schools.

Shober et al. (2006) sought to uncover the factors that influence the degree of flexibility and accountability in state charter school laws, and to determine how the content and underlying values of state charter school laws affected the formation of charter schools in the United States. Their results revealed that states with more conservative officials did produce more flexible charter laws, but partisan factors were not related to law flexibility. Also, states with higher numbers of at risk students did have more flexible laws, but higher numbers of at risk students were no different than other states in terms of accountability. Flexibility in general did not appear to be a significant predictor of number of charter schools, but three components of flexibility, ease of charter application, ease of charter authorization process, and degree of local oversight were found to be significant predictors of the number of charter schools in a state.

These quantitative analyses show that a variety of factors may be associated with both a state's decision to adopt charter school legislation and the degree of flexibility that states' charter school policies contain. Interestingly, Shober et al.'s findings revealed that the easier the overall charter application and authorization process was in a state, the more charter schools that state was likely to have. The research does not examine, however, the reasons why a state would have an easier application process. It could be that state's where a partial reversion of charter school policy has occurred are more likely to have a stringent charter school application process, and thus have fewer charter schools; while states where charter school reform has experienced very little resistance have much less stringent application procedures and more charter schools. Future research should address this gap.

Charter School Politics: National Studies

A number of recent studies have examined the politics of charter schools at the national level. (DeBray-Pelot et al., 2007; Kirst, 2007; Vergari, 2007). DeBray-Pelot et al. (2007) analyzed school choice advocacy and opposition at the national level. Their findings indicate that support and opposition for school vouchers is very much ideological, and much more complex than simple left wing–right wing, or Democratic-Republican politics. DeBray-Pelot et al. identified a relatively stable, long-term coalition in opposition to vouchers, which included teachers unions, the

National School Boards Association, and groups that they identified as traditional civil rights organizations, including the National Association for the Advancement of Colored People (NAACP), and the National Urban League. While opposition to vouchers appeared to come squarely from the political Left, DeBray-Pelot et al.'s (2007) pro voucher coalition also included what they called new civil rights groups such as the Black Alliance for Educational Opportunities and Hispanic Council for Reform and Educational Options (CREO), "who were aligned with centrist, left, and right school choice supporters" (p. 216). Finally, they found that the school choice coalition had successfully used the strategy of pushing targeted programs, citing the passage in Congress of the District of Columbia's pilot voucher program and the Hurricane Education Recovery Act in 2005 in the aftermath of Hurricane Katrina as evidence, both "significant departures from the logjams of the past" (p. 224).

DeBray-Pelot et al. (2007) framed their study as "an updated analysis of the institutional and organizational landscape surrounding the advocacy of and opposition to vouchers and other forms of school choice...at the federal/national, state, and local levels" (p. 204). They provided a framework for analyzing school voucher advocacy and opposition at the national level. This national framework, however, may not be applicable to state-level analysis because of variations in state policies. Furthermore, they point out that the coalitions identified are "loosely configured," and that all school choice supporters will not align themselves around the same school choice policies.

Kirst (2007) cautioned that generalized patterns of charter school politics may not be discernable due to diverse politics in the 50 states and thousands of localities, which vary along age composition; size of school-age population; parents' education and income; and human, material, and economic resources. Additionally, the term charter school has come to include schools that are new start-up charters, conversion from traditional public school charters, home-based charters, collective bargaining charters, and for-profit charters just to name a few. Given the different types of charter schools and diverse policy environments, different political responses arise. For example, teacher unions have been consistently noted in the research literature as opponents of charter school form, but teacher union responses alone to charter schools have ranged from complete opposition, to unions organizing for charter school teachers. In 1996, the NEA launched a charter school initiative with plans to develop five charter schools; and in 2005, the United Federation of Teachers (UFT) in New York opened the UFT Elementary Charter School in Brooklyn (Vergari, 2007; Stulberg, 2007). The differences in teacher union responses may be in part attributable to the great variation in what is meant across states by the term charter school, but also to variations in the political cultures of states (Fusarelli, 2003; Kirst, 2007).

Political culture, as defined by Elazar (1984), is a "particular pattern of political action in which each political system is imbedded" (p. 85). Citing the work of Elazar (1984), Kirst (2007) argued that states' political cultures are extremely important determinants in how states had responded and will respond to charter school reform. Elazar (1984) identified three distinctive state political cultures: a traditionalistic culture, in which government continues along traditional paternalistic and hierarchical patterns; an individualistic culture, in which government "emphasizes the centrality of private concerns and places a premium on limiting community intervention" (p. 94); and a moralistic culture, where government is seen as an "effort to exercise power for the betterment of the commonwealth" (p. 96).

Kirst (2007) asserted that traditionalistic states would most likely enact restrictive and limited charter school laws, and that individualistic states would probably enact laws that encourage charter school expansion. However, generalizations about state political culture are extremely difficult to make. Even in Elazar's (1984) attempt to categorize states, he noted that combinations of different cultures can exist within states and emphasized that migration patterns and ideological evolution contribute to an environment where states' political cultures are always in flux. Fusarelli (2003) also used Elazar's theory of political culture as a lens for examining charter school politics. Fusarelli noted that while undeniable patterns in states' political cultures exist, one limitation of Elazar's framework in explaining state responses to charter schools is that most states (41 and the District of Columbia) have passed charter school legislation, including states with identified individualistic and traditionalistic political cultures.

Charter School Politics: State Studies

Charter school politics research has also been conducted at the state level. These studies show that variations in state charter school policies and state institutional structures make it nearly impossible to make national generalizations about charter school advocacy or opposition. For instance, comparing the political construction of charter schools in Arizona, Michigan, and Georiga, Bulkley (2005) found differences among the states in terms of the political environments in which charter school legislation achieved passage, how each state's educational "problem" was defined, and each state's theory of how charter schools would fix or at least aid in fixing that problem. At the time of charter school legislation adoption in Arizona there was extremely strong support for vouchers and public school choice stemming from discontent with traditional public schools. This mood for change left moderates including professional educator organizations not incredibly resistant to the charter school idea. Charter school advocates in Arizona believed that the introduction of charter school legislation allowing for multiple sponsors/authorizers, choice, and deregulation would have effects at both the school level and system level. At the school level, they believed the new reform would ultimately result in charter schools with improved student outcomes, which were more efficient and responsive to parents. At the system level, advocates believed that allowing multiple authorizers would result in a large number of charter schools, takings students away from traditional public schools; forcing traditional public schools to improve student outcomes, and become more responsive to parents.

In Michigan, Bulkley (2005) found that charter school legislation "shows a reliance on both markets and government to connect charter schools to improved educational equality" (p. 541). Voters in Michigan were discontent with perceived abuse of power by teachers unions, inadequate school funding, and the substantial achievement gap between suburban White students and urban minority students. Charter schools came to life in Michigan as a result of the traditional public education establishment's intense opposition to open enrollment, which the Michigan Education Association (MEA) perceived to be a direct attack on public education. Additionally, Bulkley (2005) noted that some Republican legislators would not consider open enrollment because of concerns of their constituents who believed that "all the black children from Detroit would be coming up to ruin [their] schools" (p. 541). When it became evident that open enrollment was not politically feasible, the governor put all efforts and focus on charter schools.

Like Arizona, Michigan's charter school advocates believed that at the system level, multiple sponsors of charter schools would result in many charter schools taking students away from traditional public schools, and forcing traditional public schools to improve and compete with charter schools for students (Bulkley, 2005). At the school level, they believed that allowing multiple charter school authorizers in the state would contribute to greater school autonomy and more of a focus on student outcomes than if local school boards were the only potential authorizers. Also, charter advocates believed that charter schools that were able to overcome all of the obstacles of starting a school from nothing would be higher quality schools.

Finally, in Georgia, neither parental choice, nor competition were a part of the charter school conversation (Bulkley, 2005). At the time of charter school legislation adoption in Georgia, the most discussed education problems were low teacher pay, increasing state control of public education, and an ongoing struggle between state and local control of public schools. Solutions being considered included raising teacher pay, and forms of site-based management. Georgia's charter school legislation allowed only existing public schools to apply to the State Board of Education and local school to substitute a charter for exemption from many state and local regulations. Students who attended the school as a traditional public school would continue in attendance. There was no element of parental choice in Georgia's legislation. Charter school advocates in Georgia intended that decreased regulation by the state would result in more school autonomy, which in turn would yield higher performing public schools. If any systemic benefit was intended to come from charter legislation, it was only that traditional public schools might learn from innovations experimented with by charter schools.

The passage of charter school legislation in Minnesota came about with the support of both of the state's teachers unions. Interestingly, the concept of charter schools in Minnesota, the first state to adopt charter school legislation, is quite different than the market-model charter school. Rather, charter schools were intended to give teachers greater control and authority in schools, not parents (DiConti, 1996). The initial law, passed in 1991, allowed only groups of teachers to form "totally autonomous schools of choice within existing school buildings with the right to decide on the curriculum, the allocation of funds, and the hiring and retention of staff" (DiConti, 1996, p. 100). Charter school advocates in Minnesota argued that increasing teacher control in schools would result in greater curricular and instructional innovations, and provide high-quality learning opportunities for more students. Teachers unions who had not been receptive to Minnesota's past forays with school choice policies saw charter school legislation as a tremendous opportunity for both teachers and students. The only noted opposition to charter school legislation in Minnesota was not even an objection to charter schools themselves. Instead, some educators opposed charter schools because they believed that they were a step in the direction of introducing private school vouchers.

Stulberg (2007) described the politics of charter schools in New York during what she called the second generation of charter schools as "incredibly complex" (p. 1). Again, this state-level analysis illustrated that generalizations often made about charter school support and opposition do not always hold true. Though teachers unions have been painted with the broad brush of being anti-charter, Stulberg (2007) asserted that there is a great deal of disagreement within the state teachers union, "evidenced by the fact that there are unionized charter schools in New York State" (p. 3). Stulberg found that a major sticking point was between supporters who wanted to be able to claim the superiority of charter schools and opponents who wished to show that charter school performance is subpar or no better than traditional public schools. Evidence of this disagreement is seen nationally as well, with findings of charter school effects varying across studies (Vergari, 2007).

Stulberg (2007) maintained that school district responses to charter schools have varied across the state of New York. Much of the literature has characterized local school districts as fierce opponents of charter schools. Some school districts in New York, for example, opposed charter schools and felt deeply threatened by their presence. However, she also found school districts that either embraced charter schools or believed that charters were "not an issue in their communities" (p. 4). Stulberg's findings of variation in local district responses to charter schools brings us to caution even generalizations about patterns of support and opposition at the state level. Differences between charter school politics in New York City and Albany, New York, must be taken into account in describing New York's unique political landscape. Leaving those types of contrasts out of political analyses would only serve to oversimplify a very complex issue.

In analyzing charter school support and opposition in Texas, Fusarelli (2003) found that charter school legislation was "a byproduct of the competition between advocacy groups" (p. 93). Bipartisan support in the legislature, the support of Republican and Democratic governors, the mobilization of various advocacy groups in support of charter schools, and the inability of charter school opponents to successfully countermobilize, all contributed to the fairly easy passage of Texas charter school legislation in 1995.

Fusarelli (2003) also found evidence of the impact of institutional structures on the school choice politics. These structures included restrictions in the state constitution that prohibited the support of religious schools with public funding, the length and frequency of legislative sessions, and the constitutional authority of state executive and legislative leadership. While institutional structure will rarely independently determine policy outcomes, "it does serve as a conditioner of the political processes by which those policy outcomes are achieved" (Fusarelli, 2003, p. 70). Thus, discussing charter school politics or state-level politics in general is only meaningful when considered within the context of each state's unique institutional landscape.

Texas' original charter school legislation allowed for 20 state-approved open-enrollment charter schools and an unlimited number of district-approved campus charter schools (Fusarelli, 2002). The Texas legislature increased the cap to 120 open-enrollment charters and an unlimited number of additional charter schools provided that each additional school's student body be comprised of at least 75% of students at risk of dropping out. And in 2001, the legislature increased the cap again to 215 charter schools statewide, with an exemption only for schools run by a state college or university. It is apparent that since the passage of Texas' initial charter school legislation, charter school advocates have been successful with continuing to raise the charter school cap, and expand the number of charter schools in the state. At first glance, it appears that traditional public school interests in Texas have not been able to force a policy reversion. Fusarelli (2002) noted, however, that a significant portion of the growth in Texas charter schools has been with a targeted population—at risk students, and Texas charter schools continue to operate under the same accountability system as traditional public schools. Both of which could be viewed as victories for traditional public school interests. Further research would need to be conducted to determine whether charter school advocates have established a new status quo, or the traditional public education establishment's once policy monopoly has broken down into an issue network.

Similarly, changes in Colorado's charter school policy since the passage of the state's original legislation warrant further investigation. Colorado's initial charter school law passed the state legislature in 1993 with bipartisan support as well as the support of the state's teachers unions (Hirsch, 2002). Much of its appeal was its limited scope. The law allowed only the local school districts to approve charter school applications, permitted school districts to negotiate funding levels with charter schools (with a minimum of 80% of the district's per pupil operating revenue), required charter schools to negotiate any waivers from local and state policies, provided a sunset provision of five years, capped the number of charter schools at 60, and required that 16 of the 60 charter schools be designed to serve at risk students. Since 1993, numerous changes have been made to Colorado's charter school law. Some of the most notable changes have been the removal of the sunset provision, significant increases in minimum funding levels including improvement in capital funding. Charter school advocates have been unsuccessful, however, with getting a bill through the state legislature that would allow entities other than school districts to authorize charter schools. In addition to this limitation being a sticking point during the charter application, the charter authorizer is responsible for oversight of approved charter schools. Further investigation is needed to determine whether or not a reversion of charter school policy in Colorado has occurred.

Charter School Policy: State Snapshots

There is no better illustration of the diversity of charter school policies across the United States than snapshots of charter school policies from the various states. The Center for Education Reform (CER) gives a letter grade—A, B, C, D, or F—for each state's charter school law. According to its 2012 report and rankings of charter school laws across the United States, CER's methodology for ranking is based on "what exists in law, in regulation, in administrative guidance—and how such laws and regulations work for or against charter schools" (Center for Education Reform, 2012, p. 5). In order to illustrate the substantial diversity of charter school laws across the country I have used CER's charter school law grade report for selecting a sample of state charter school laws to highlight in this section.

CER (2012) asserts that there are four critical components to determining the development and creation of high-quality and autonomous charter schools within a state; these include the existence of multiple independent charter school authorizers, the number of schools allowed to operate, operational and fiscal autonomy, and equitable funding (p. 6). A few of CER's charter school policy positions are that (a) state laws should provide multiple authorization paths for charter schools, (b) laws should not place restrictions on the number of charter schools that may operate within a state—for example, no caps on the number of charter schools that may operate within a state or district, or on the number of charter schools that may be authorized in a year, (c) laws should ensure that charter schools are able to operate relatively autonomously with regard to both school operations and fiscal autonomy, and (d) laws should ensure that charter schools are funded equitably with traditional public schools, this applies to funding from both state and local sources.

CER evaluates each state's law according to a rubric assessing and awards points to each of these identified policy areas. A state's law may earn up to 55 points, with each area weighted as follows: (a) independent/multiple authorizers (15 points), (b) number of schools allowed (10 points), (c) operational independence (15 points), and (d) funding equity (15 points).

In the following subsections I provide overviews of charter school laws in the following states: District of Columbia, which received a grade of A; Ohio, which received a grade of B; North Carolina, which received a grade of C; Wyoming, which received a grade of D; and Mississippi, which received a grade of F. The purpose for selecting state laws in this fashion is not to give support or discredit CER's grading methodology, neither is the purpose to analyze every detail of charter school laws in the selected states. Instead, my intent is to provide the reader with a sampling of state laws, illustrating the enormous variation in how states have defined charter schools, the application procedures states have developed, the number and variation in charter school authorizers across the states, the states' mechanisms for holding charter schools accountable, and the degree of autonomy that charter school legislation grants to charter schools across the states.

District of Columbia

As of January 2013, the District of Columbia (DC) had a total of 110 charter schools in operation. The CER graded the DC's charter school law as an A in 2012, awarding it 46 out of 50 points and ranking it as the number one charter school law in the United States. DC's initial charter school legislation was passed in 1996. Public charter schools in DC are defined by law as publicly funded schools that are not part of the DC public schools. Eligible applicant for establishing a charter school in DC may include "a person, including a private, public, or quasi-public entity, or an institution of higher education."

DC's charter school law specifies two eligible chartering authorities (authorizers): the DC Board of Education and the Public Charter School Board. In 2006, the DC Board of Education voted to relinquish its authority for authorizing charter schools; their authorizing authority has since been given to the state education agency (SEA). Legislation passed in 2007 gave the mayor of DC authority over the traditional public school system and transferred the oversight responsibilities for charter schools that were authorized by the DC Board of Education to the DC Public Charter School Board (PCSB).

Boards
Governing boards for DC charter schools are termed boards of trustees. The members of boards are to be selected pursuant to the guidelines provided in the school's charter.

Ohio

As of January 2013, Ohio had a total of 395 charter schools in operation. The CER graded Ohio's charter school law as a B in 2012, awarding it a total of 30 out of 55 points, and ranking it as the fifteenth best charter school law in the United States. Charter school legislation was passed in Ohio in 1997 with the first schools opening in 1998. Charter schools in Ohio are called community schools, and defined as "a public school, independent of any school district, and is part of the state's program of education." The law exempts charter schools "from all state laws and rules pertaining to schools, school districts, and boards of education, except those laws and rules that grant certain rights to parents." Since the enactment of Ohio's initial charter school law, the law has been amended pretty regularly and sometimes in rather significant ways. This overview of Ohio's law is current as of January 2013.

Ohio's law allows for the conversion of traditional public schools into charter schools and for the establishment of start-up charter schools. Any person or group may submit a proposal for the conversion of a traditional public school into a charter school. Proposals for conversion must be made to the local board of education where the school is located; or if the school is operated by an educational service center, the proposal must be submitted to the governing board of the service center. The local board of education or the educational service center that enters into contract with the conversion school becomes the sponsor of the school.

Start-up charter schools in Ohio may be proposed by any person or group. Start-ups may only be created, however, in districts designated as *challenged school districts*. Challenged school districts include any of the following: (a) a district ranked in the bottom 5% of school districts in Ohio based on its state Performance Index Score; (b) a district rated as *Academic Emergency* or *Academic Watch*; (c) one of the state's largest eight school districts—Akron, Canton, Cincinnati, Cleveland, Columbus, Dayton, Toledo, and Youngstown; or (d) a district in the state's Lucas County charter school pilot project area.

Authorizer, Sponsors and Accountability
The Ohio State Board of Education serves as authorizer of charter school sponsors. Eligible charter school sponsors in Ohio include the Ohio Department of Education; local boards of education; the sponsoring authority designated by the Board of Trustees of any of the following state universities—The University of Akron, Bowling Green State, Central State, University of Cincinnati, Cleveland State, Kent State, Miami, Ohio, Ohio State, Shawnee State, University of Toledo, Wright State, and Youngstown State; governing boards of educational service centers, and a nonprofit organization that (a) has operated for at least five years prior to applying for sponsorship, (b) has assets of at least $500,000 and a record of financial responsibility, and (c) has been determined by the Ohio Department of Education to be an "education-oriented entity" with a record of successfully delivering educational program.

Ohio's charter school law includes some of the strongest performance accountability measures in the United States, including provisions for the automatic closure of charter schools. Students in Ohio charter schools are subject to the same state testing requirements as their counterparts in traditional public schools, and may be even be subject to additional requirements depending on what the school has agreed on with its sponsoring entity. Each governing board of an Ohio charter school is required to submit the following to its sponsors and the parents of all students enrolled in the school: (a) a full report of the school's activities including the progress it is making toward meeting its specific goals and performance standards and (b) a report of the school's financial status. A school that fails to meet performance expectations may be subject to probation, charter expiration, charter termination, or charter nonrenewal by the school's sponsoring entity. With a change to the law in 2011, a charter school *will* be permanently closed for consistently low ratings and a failure to make adequate academic growth. For schools serving students up to grade 3, automatic closure is triggered if a school is in *academic emergency* for two of the past three years. For schools serving students in grades 4 through 8, automatic closure is triggered if a school is in *academic emergency* for two of the past three years, and it has demonstrated less than one year of academic growth in reading or math for two of the past three years. For schools serving students in grades 10 through 12, automatic closure is triggered if a school is in *academic emergency* for two of the past three years. Schools' ratings during their first two years of operation, however, are not a part of calculations for automatic closure assessment. Also, exemptions to the automatic closure rules include schools with approved dropout recovery school waivers and schools in which the majority of students receive special education and related services.

Boards
Ohio's charter school law has specific requirements of boards and board members for start-up charter schools. A board may vote to compensate its members for service on the board. Board members, however, may receive no more than $5,000 in compensation from all boards on which they serve, and no more than $425 per meeting. The law requires that boards have a minimum of five members, with none of the members owing the state money or be involved in a dispute with the state about whether money is owed related to the operation of a charter school. Board members may serve on no more than two start-up boards at a time, and neither board members nor their immediate relatives (including spouses, children, parents, grandparents, siblings, and in-laws) may work for a charter school operator for one year following the end of board membership.

Admissions

Ohio charter schools must be open to any student eligible to attend a public school in Ohio, and they may not restrict admissions based on race, gender, creed, color, or disability status. Charter schools may restrict admissions based on grade levels, age groups, "at risk" students, and geographical resident. Additionally, the law does permit for the creation of single-gender charter schools as long as there are comparable offerings for male and female students.

If a school receives more applications than seats available, the requires that a lottery be held based on the students who submitted applications for admissions. The law requires that preference in the lottery be given to students residing in the *home* district and students who attended the school the previous year (conversion charter schools). The law permits schools to give preference to siblings of students who attended the school the previous year.

Teachers

Teachers in conversion charter schools remain part of the converting school district's collective bargaining unit unless a majority of the teachers at the converting school vote otherwise. The law makes an exception, however, for teachers in conversion charter schools in the Cleveland Metropolitan School District: The mayor may submit to the Cleveland Board of Education and to the state employee relations board a request that employees of a conversion school in Cleveland be removed from the collective bargaining agreement.

North Carolina

As of January 2013, North Carolina had a total of 114 charter schools in operation. The CER graded North Carolina's charter school law as a C in 2012, awarding it 22 out of 55 points and ranking it as the twenty-second best law in the country. Charter schools in North Carolina were created with the passage of House Bill 955 during the 1996 session of the North Carolina General Assembly. This legislation's stated purposes were to:

> Improve student learning, increase learning opportunities for all students, with special emphasis on expanded learning experiences for students who are identified as at risk of academic failure or academically gifted, encourage the use of different and innovative teaching methods, create new professional development opportunities for teachers, including the opportunities to be responsible for the learning program at the school site, provide parents and students with expanded choices in the types

of educational opportunities that are available within the public school system, and hold the schools established under this Part accountable for meeting measurable student achievement results, and provide the schools with a method to change from rule-based to performance-based accountability systems.

North Carolina charter schools are operated by private nonprofit corporations with federal tax-exempt status. The state's charter school law allows for the establishment of charter schools as public schools, held accountable for compliance with applicable laws and the standards of performance agreed upon in their respective charters by either the local board of education where the school is located or the State Board of Education. North Carolina charter schools are exempt from many statutes and rules applicable to local school districts. The law initially allowed the State Board of Education to grant charters to no more than one hundred schools statewide. That statutory cap on charter schools was removed in 2011.

Any person, group of persons, or nonprofit corporation may submit an application to establish a charter school in North Carolina. The law permits both the establishment of start-up charter schools and the conversion of traditional public schools into charters. For applicants wishing to convert a traditional public school to a charter, the proposal must include a statement signed by a majority of the school's current teachers and instructional support personnel indicating their wish to convert as well as evidence that a "significant number" of parents of children enrolled support the conversion.

Charter School Advisory Committee
North Carolina's charter school law authorized the State Board of Education to establish a Charter School Advisory Committee for the purpose of implementation of the charter school law. Statute stipulates that this committee may serve in the following capacities: (a) provide technical assistance to chartering entities and charter applicants; (b) review applications for preliminary approval; (c) make recommendations to the State Board for approval or disapproval of charter school applications; (d) make recommendations to the State Board for the renewal or termination of a charter; (e) make recommendations concerning grievances between charter schools and chartering entities, the State Board, or local boards of education; (f) assist with the review and evaluation of the "educational effectiveness of the charter school approach" and the impact of charter schools on traditional public schools in the areas where charter schools are located; and (g) "provide any other assistance as may be required by the State Board."

Authorizers and Accountability
North Carolina's law created three chartering entities in the state with the authority to give preliminary approval to charter schools: local boards of education, the board of trustees of a constituent institution of the University of North Carolina (with the provision that this institution is involved in the planning, operation or evaluation of the charter school), and the State Board of Education. Chartering entities are authorized to give preliminary approval to charter applications, but final approval for all charter schools rests solely with the State Board of Education. Applicants who are denied preliminary approval by a chartering entity other than the State Board of Education may appeal to the State Board. The State Board may give preliminary approval to an application on appeal if it finds that the chartering entity "acted in an arbitrary or capricious manner in disapproving the application, failed to consider appropriately the application, or failed to act within the time set" by law.

If a charter applicant submits an application to a chartering entity other than the local board of education, within seven days of its application, the applicant must also submit a copy of its application to the local board of education where the charter school will be located. The local board may offer comments or information about the application to the chartering entity. The law requires that when making decisions about preliminary or final approval of a charter application, the State Board will consider the information or comments submitted by the local board of education, and consider the "impact on the local school administrative unit's ability to provide a sound basic education to its students." The State Board may grant initial charters for periods of up to ten years, and upon the request of a chartering entity, may renew charters for subsequent periods of up to ten years.

For the purposes of ensuring compliance with laws and meeting the standards agreed upon in their respective charters, North Carolina charter schools are held accountable to either the local board of education (if it applied for and received preliminary approval from that local board) or to the State Board of Education. Any charter school, however, may choose to be held accountable to local board of education where the charter school operates instead of the State Board. The law requires that each charter school report at least annually to its chartering entity and the State Board of Education the information required by the chartering entity or the State Board. The State Board is required by statute to review each charter school's operations at least once every five years to ensure that the school is meeting academic, financial, and governance expectations. The State Board or the chartering entity (subject to approval by the State Board) may terminate or not renew a schools charter for any of the following reasons: (a) failure to meet the requirements for student performance contained in the charter; (b) failure to meet generally accepted standards for fiscal management; (c) violations of the law; (d) "material violation" of the standards, conditions, and procedures set forth in the school's charter; (e) two-thirds of the faculty and instructional support personnel request that the charter be terminated or not renewed; or (f) other good identified causes.

Local school districts are not required to, but may provide administrative and evaluative assistance to charter schools located within their boundaries. Private persons and organizations may provide funding or assistance to charter schools. Through the Office of Charter Schools, created by the charter school law, the North Carolina Department of Public Instruction (NCDPI) provides guidance and technical assistance to charter schools and applicants for charters.

Boards

Boards of directors for charter schools must be approved by the State Board at the time of charter approval. As part of the charter application, applicants are required to explain the proposed governance structure for the school, including the names of the school's proposed initial board of directors. The law grants to charter school boards the authority to make operations decisions for the school, including budgeting, curriculum, and operating procedures.

Facilities

North Carolina charter schools do not receive funding for facilities. North Carolina's law does permit charter schools to lease space from local boards of education or from public or private nonsectarian organizations. The law prohibits charter schools from using funds allocated by the state to purchase land or buildings, and only permits charter schools to purchase land and buildings with funds obtained through non-state funding sources. Amendments to the initial law passed in 1997 allow charter schools to lease space from sectarian organizations, providing that no religious artifacts were visible. Additionally, the amendments compel local school districts to consider leasing buildings to charter schools. Local boards of education of the local school administrative units where charter schools are located are directed to lease any available building or land to charter schools. Only local boards that demonstrate that leasing facilities is not economically or practically feasible or that the local board does not have adequate classroom space to meet its enrollment needs are permitted to refuse facilities to charter schools. Additionally, for new charter schools that are unable to find adequate facilities in the local school district where the school was approved to operate, the amendments allow the

State Board of Education to authorize a charter school to operate within a neighboring county for a one-year period. Subsequent to that one-year period, however, the charter school would be required to reapply for a charter and receive final approval from the State Board of Education to continue operating in that county.

Funding
North Carolina charter schools receive both state and local funds. The law directs the State Board of Education to allocate to charter schools "an amount equal to the average daily membership from the local school administrative unit allotments in which the charter school is located for each child attending the charter school." Charter schools receive additional funding for students with disabilities and students with limited English proficiency. The law also directs the local school district where the child resides to "transfer to the charter school an amount equal to the per pupil local current expense appropriation to the local school administrative unit for the fiscal year." Pertaining to local funds, however, funds from revenue derived from local supplemental taxes are only to be transferred to charter schools located in the tax district where the taxes are collected and in which the student resides.

Teachers
North Carolina's charter school law does not require that all teachers employed by charter schools hold valid North Carolina teaching certificates. Instead, the law requires that in each charter school, at least 75% of teachers in grades kindergarten, at least 50% of teachers in grades 6 through 8, and at least 50% of teachers in grades 9 through 12 "shall hold teacher certificates." The law further requires that any teacher teaching in grades 6 through 12 in one of the core academic areas of math, science, social studies, and language arts, have a college degree. Finally, as collective bargaining for public sector employees is illegal in North Carolina, the state's charter school law does not address collective bargaining agreements between local boards of education and teachers unions and the impact of such agreements on teachers at charter schools. The does stipulate, however, that "education employee associations shall have equal access to charter school employees."

Wyoming

As of January 2013, Wyoming had a total of five charter schools in operation. The CER graded Wyoming's law as a D in 2012, awarding it a total 13 out of 55 points. According to Wyoming's law, charter schools legislation was intended to provide teachers, parents, students, and community members with opportunities to establish and maintain schools for the purposes of improving student learning; increasing learning opportunities for students, with emphasis on "expanded learning opportunities"; expanding professional opportunities for teachers; and expanding school choices for students and families. The law prohibits the conversion of private schools into charter schools. A Wyoming charter school is required to be a "public, nonsectarian, nonreligious, non-home-based school which operates within a public school district."

The law does not specifically waive any policies and regulations for charter schools, but provides for the possibility of waivers pursuant to the details of a charter school's individual contract. According to the statute:

> Pursuant to the contract, a charter school may operate free from specified school district policies and state regulations. Pursuant to contract, a school district may waive locally imposed school district requirements, without seeking approval of the state board. The state board may waive state statutory requirements or rules promulgated by the stats by the board, except that the state board shall not waive any statute or rule relating to the assessments or standards required to be administered...Any waiver of state statutes or local district regulations made pursuant to this subsection shall be for the term of the charter for which the waiver is made, except that a waiver of state statutes or regulations by the state board shall be subject to review every two (2) years and may be revoked if the waiver is deemed no longer necessary by the state board.

Wyoming law establishes three types of charter schools: charter schools within schools, converted charter schools, and new charter schools. New charter schools are defined as charter schools "established within the district which is located in a facility or a portion of a facility which is not currently being operated by the district as a public school." Converted charter schools are defined as charter schools "converted from an existing public school operating within the district." Charter schools within schools are defined as a charter school "operating within a facility or portion of a facility currently operated by the district as a public school or operated as an adjunct to a public school or schools with students attending both the charter school and the public school."

Applications
An application for a new charter school may be made to the local board of education by any person. Applications to convert an existing public school into a charter school may be made by "administrators and teachers employed by the district, parents of students enrolled in the district and

any special district advisory group comprised of district residents." The application to convert a public school into a charter school must have the documented support of 50% of the teachers employed by the school to be converted and the parents of 50% of all students attending the school. A district board and a charter school applicant may jointly apply to establish a charter school within a school, which would operate as a separate school and have the rights and responsibilities any other Wyoming charter school.

An application for a charter school is to be a proposed agreement between the applicant and the local board of education. The application is to include but is not limited to: (a) a description of the school's educational program; (b) "the measurable pupil outcomes identified for use by the charter school" (such outcomes must include state assessments and standards); (c) a description of how students' academic progress is to measured; (d) a description of the governance structure for the school, including plans for ensure parent, teacher, and community involvement; (e) a description of the required qualifications to be met by employees; (f) procedures for ensuring health and safety in the school; (g) procedures for annual audit of financial operations; (h) school discipline policies and procedures; (i) minimum enrollment requirements; (j) evidence that the school's plan is "economically sound"; (k) a plan for the displacement of students and teachers who will not remain at the charter school; (l) "an explanation of the relationship that will exist between the proposed charter school and employees, including evidence that the terms and conditions of employment have been addressed with affected employees and their recognized representatives"; and (m) a description of how the school will meet students' transportation needs and whether it will provide transportation for students. Local boards of education may grant charters for periods of not more than five years, and may renew charters for successive periods of not more than five years.

Accountability
A charter school is a public school within the school district that grants its charter and it is held accountable to the local board of education for purposes of ensuring compliance with applicable laws, the provisions of its charter, and the requirements of the state constitution. All charter schools are required to meet the Wyoming uniform educational program standards imposed upon public schools and the uniform state student content and performance standards required by the State Board of Education, including requirements for state assessments.

Applications to the local board of education for the renewal of a school's charter must include: (a) a report on the school's progress in achieving its goals, objectives, pupil performance standards, content standards, and terms agreed upon in the school's charter, and (b) a financial statement disclosing costs of administration, instruction, and other spending categories. Local boards of education may choose to revoke or not renew if the board determines that a charter school has done any of the following: (a) committed a material violation of the terms of the charter; (b) "failed to meet or make reasonable progress toward achievement of the content standards or pupil performance standards identified in the charter application"; (c) failed to meet standards of fiscal management; or (d) violated provisions of state statutes or regulations or district regulations from which the charter school was not exempted. Further, a local board may choose to not renew a charter if it determines that "it is not in the interest of the pupils residing within the school district to continue the operation of the charter school."

Charter schools may appeal the denial, revocation, or nonrenewal decisions of the local board of education to the State Board of Education. Charter schools are required to "limit the grounds of the appeal to the grounds for denial specified by the district board." If the State Board of Education finds that local board of education's decision was "contrary to the best interests of the pupils, school district or community, the state board shall remand such decision to the district board with written instructions for reconsideration thereof."

Boards
Wyoming's law requires charter schools to be "administered and governed" by a governing board "in a manner agreed to by the charter school applicant and the school district."

Funding
Charter schools may receive funding from private persons and organizations providing that the local board of education "determines the funding or assistance is compatible with the mission of the district."

Facilities
Wyoming charter schools may negotiate with the school district or a third party for the use of facilities and grounds. Charter schools may not be required to pay rent to school districts for space deemed to be "available" in district facilities. Costs associated with improvement, modification, operation, and maintenance, however, "shall be subject to negotiation between the charter school and the district board." Charter school contracts must specify that upon a charter school's closure, all charter school assets purchased with public funds become the property of the school district.

Teachers

Teachers in Wyoming charter schools must meet the same requirements for certification by the Wyoming professional teaching standards board and any other qualifications required of teaches to teach in Wyoming public schools.

Mississippi

As of January 2013, Mississippi had no charter schools in operation. The CER graded Mississippi's law as an F in 2012, awarding it a total 1 out of 55 points. Of note, the Mississippi state legislature passed new charter school legislation in April 2013. This discussion, however, is of Mississippi's charter school law as of January 2013. Mississippi's charter school law was passed initially in 2010 as the Charter Conversion Act of 2010. The law defines a conversion charter school as "a public school that has converted to operating under the terms of a contract entered into between the local management board of a conversion charter school and the State Board of Education." Mississippi's law places limits on the number of schools the State Board of Education may approve. The State Board may approve up to 12 conversion charter schools during the period from 2010 until 2016, and no more than three petitions for charters in each of the state's four congressional districts may be approved. No conversion charter schools were to begin operations before July 2013. Start-up charter schools may not be authorized under this law.

The Mississippi law defines a petition as "a proposal to enter into an academic or vocational, or both, performance-based contract between the State Board of Education and the sponsors of a local school whereby the local school obtains a conversion charter school status." Charter school sponsors in Mississippi may be a group of parents and guardians of students enrolled in a public school designated as *low-performing, at risk of failing,* or failing, or an organization that has been appointed or selected to represent those parents or guardians. The petition and the plan for school conversion must be approved by more than 50% of the families of students enrolled in the school, with each family receiving one vote regardless of the number of children from that family attending the school.

Successful petitions for conversion must include the following: (a) a plan for school improvement, including improvement of student learning and achieving a higher rating in the state's school accountability model; (b) a set of academic and/or vocational "performance-based objectives and student achievement-based objectives for the term of the contract and the means for measuring those objectives on no less than an annual basis"; (c) an agreement to provide annual reports of the school's progress to the local board of education, parents, and the State Board of Education; (d) an agreement that the school will remain nonsectarian; (e) an agreement that the school will not charge for tuition; and (f) an agreement that the school will be subject to financial audits in the same manner as traditional public schools.

Along with petitions for conversions, sponsors must submit conversion plans. The law requires conversion plans to include the following: (a) a description of the school's plan for school improvement that specifically addresses how the school proposes to work toward improving student learning and achieving a higher rating in the state's accountability model; (b) "an outline of proposed academic or vocational, or both, performance criteria to be used during the initial period of the contract to measure progress of the school in improving student learning and achieving a Successful rating or higher under the State Accountability Model," including: (i) requirements academic performance criteria include specific and measurable benchmarks for student performance on state assessment, and a requirement that schools not miss AYP or other future federal school accountability requirements for any two consecutive years and (ii) a provision requiring the school to comply with all rules, regulations, policies and procedures of the State Board of Education and the local school board and the provisions of the Mississippi Code of 1972 relating to the elementary and secondary education of students, except those rules, regulations, policies or procedures from which the conversion charter school specifically requests to be exempted and which have been agreed upon by the State Board of Education as specified in the school's contract.

Additionally, before submission of the petition to the State Board of Education, the sponsor is required to conduct a public hearing in the local school district where the school is located.

The law authorizes the Mississippi State Board of Education to accept petitions according to a timeline to be developed by the State Board, rate all petitions according to criteria to be developed by the State Board, with the criteria to include "criteria relating to improving student performance and encouraging new and innovative programs." After providing initial ratings for petitions, "with the advice of the Commission on School Accreditation," the State Board will approve or deny petitions based on its criteria. The Mississippi State Board of Education is authorized to issue contracts for conversion charter schools for a minimum three-year term, and may renew conversion charter school contracts for up to three years provided that "all parties to the original contract" approve renewal with a majority vote of parents or guardians of students enrolled in the school. However, after three years as a conversion charter school, parents or guardians of students enrolled in the school may request that conversion charter school status be removed from the school by submitting a petition to the State Board of Education with the support of over 50% of the school's parents or guardians.

Mississippi's conversion charter schools continue to function as traditional public schools in the most ways. Conversion charter schools continue receive funding and are provided with transportation services in the same manner that these were provided before receiving conversion charter status. In addition to state and local funding, the law permits conversion charter schools to receive additional funds from other public or private sources. In fact, the law goes to great lengths to make it quite clear that conversion charter schools may receive funds from the federal Race to the Top program. The following excerpt from the law strongly suggests that the passage of Mississippi's Conversion Charter School Act of 2010 was in large part an effort to win federal Race to the Top Funds:

> It is the intent of the Legislature that in accordance with the conditions of federal funding under the federal "Race to the Top" program, public schools converted to conversion charter school status in Mississippi are authorized to operate conversion charter and autonomous public school programs that are high-performing. It is further the intent of the Legislature that public schools converted to conversion charter schools receive equitable state and federal funding compared to traditional public schools, as required by the federal "Race to the Top" program, and that the state shall not impose any school facility-related requirements on conversion charter schools which are more restrictive than those applied to traditional public schools.

Children in the attendance zone of a conversion charter school prior to the conversion continue to attend the conversion charter school after the conversion. Conversion charter schools are only open for the enrollment of transfer students from another school if openings are available. When seats are available in a conversion charter school, the local management board is required to establish an application process for children who reside in the school district but outside of the school's attendance zone. The local board of education does not provide transportation services for students outside the attendance zone who are admitted to the conversion charter school. If, however, a parent chooses not to send her child to the school after conversion, the local board of education will permit the student to attend another school in the district; and if a district alternative is not available, the local board will give the student a release to seek enrollment in another district.

Boards

The governing board of charter school in Mississippi is designated by law the *local management board*. This board consists of five members and is composed of parents or guardians of students enrolled in the conversion charter school. The parents or guardians of students enrolled in a conversion charter school are required to select members for the local management board according to procedures to be promulgated by the State Board of Education. The local management board is charges with responsibility for "the academic and administrative functions and decisions" of the school, with the academic functions, however, "subject to the authority of the local school board." The law extends civil and criminal immunity to the individual members of local management boards for activities related to charter schools, and provides limited liability for the local management board when acting in its official capacity. The board may be held liable only for matters in which it has had direct involvement, including "the misappropriation of funds, the appropriation of funds beyond the scope of its authority, abridging the due process rights of a student attending the conversion charter school, gross negligence, intentional and willful misconduct, malfeasance and nonfeasance." Local school boards, however, are required to provide the local management board of a conversion charter school with the same legal representation the local school board would receive.

Teachers

Mississippi law stipulates that teachers and all employees in conversion charter schools are to be deemed employees of the local school district. Charter school employees are given explicit protection "unlawful reprisal" because of their direct or indirect involvement with a petition to convert a traditional public school into a conversion charter school.

Charter School Policy Variation

As the state charter school policy snapshots illustrate, charter school laws across the states vary considerably. They vary mostly by their differences in a few key areas. Those areas include (a) the number of independent authorizers the law allows; (b) the number of schools the law permits to operate at any one time; (c) the degree of school autonomy; (d) requirements for teacher certification; and (e) funding, including funds provided for facilities. As illustrated with the preceding snapshots of state charter school policies, the number of charter school authorizers may vary considerably across the states. While states like Wyoming have chosen to limit charter school authorization only to local boards of education where the charter schools is proposed to locate, other states like Ohio and North Carolina have chosen to grant authorization powers to multiple entities including local boards of education, the State Board of Education, and state universities. There is considerable variation in the number of charter schools allowed to operate within a state. While states like DC, North Carolina, Ohio, and Wyoming permit the authorization of both start-up charter schools and conversion charter schools, states like Mississippi allow that only persistently low-achieving schools may be converted to charter schools. While DC's law places no limits on the number of charters schools that may be authorized or on the number of charter schools that may be authorized by an authorizer, states like Mississippi have greatly restricted charter school growth and expansion. While states such as North Carolina allow charter schools to employ some teachers without state teaching certification, most other states' charter school laws require that teachers employed by charter schools meet the same requirements as teachers at any other public school in the state. Finally, the state snapshots show clearly that states vary considerably in the degree of autonomy granted to charter schools. States like DC, North Carolina, and Ohio grant charter schools blanket waivers from some local and state regulations, but in state's like Mississippi and Wyoming, charter schools must request waivers from specific regulations and provide justification for why such a waiver has been requested.

The variations that we find in charter school laws most often come as a result of differences in state politics. Typically, in states where parents choice policy supporters generally and charter school advocates in particular have had significant influence in the state legislature and where Republicans have held majorities in the legislature, laws have been passed and amended in ways that have been much more favorable for the establishment, expansion, funding, and autonomy of charter schools. Typically, in states where Democrats have dominated in state politics and parent choice advocates have been less successful with grassroots advocacy and mobilization, either charter school policies have not been passed or the laws on the books tend to be more restrictive of charter schools. These differences in state politics have led to very significant differences in state charter school laws. And in fact, charter school laws across the states vary so considerably across so many different policy areas that talking about charter schools across the United States as a singular concept or reform idea is unwise. Variations in the definitions of charter schools across the states sampled here alone should be enough to give even the casual policy observer pause before making generalizations about charter schools or charter school policies across states.

Charter School Policy Debate

While 40 states and the District of Columbia now have some form of charter school policy, political debate about charter schools and charter school policy remains contentious; this is true in states with and without charter school policies. One example is Kentucky, where charter school legislation has been offered in the state legislature for years but has yet to even come up for vote in the Democrat-controlled state House of Representatives. In Kentucky, as in many other states, teacher unions that oppose the passage of charter school legislation heavily fund the campaigns of Democratic legislators. That campaign funding has bought unions access to Democratic legislators, who on unions' behalf have opposed even serious consideration of the passage of a charter school policy.

While the political landscape of each state has its unique aspects, there are a few common themes that have characterized political debate over charter schools across the states. Those themes include differences of position on the issues of funding, teachers' job security, waivers from regulations for charter schools, and racial balance in schools, which is addressed is chapter 5.

A frequent criticism of charter school policy has been that charter schools divert critical funding from traditional public schools. With this issue, as with each of the issues that I will highlight here, perspective is of the utmost importance. Traditional public school advocates see state funding that would follow a child to a charter school as funding being taken away from traditional public schools; while charter school advocates make the argument that state funding is for children and not schools, so a school may only claim funding as its own if it is serving the child the funding is for. So to agree with traditional public school advocates, yes, if a student leaves a traditional public school, the funding for that student leaves the school with her and goes to the traditional public or charter school that they choose. But to also, to agree with charter school advocates, charter schools do not take funding away from traditional public schools, funding follows children to the public schools their parents choose for them.

Another prominent theme in charter school policy debate is job security for teachers. It is true that in many charter schools, teachers do not have the protections of collective bargaining agreements. It is also true, however, that most teachers in America do not have the protections of collective bargaining agreements. Teachers in charter schools are generally held to performance standards of accountability and face the possibility of being relieved of their duties if they fail to meet those performance standards. That is a standard of accountability that has not existed for teachers in traditional public schools, or private schools for that matter. But teacher accountability is a policy area that is rapidly changing for all public school teachers. Gone is the day when teachers were not evaluated in part based on the performance of their students. So whether the discussion is one of charter or traditional public school teachers, teachers who cannot show evidence of their students' growth will no longer be secure in their positions.

Charter school critics have also argued that charter schools will take jobs away from traditionally trained and certified teachers. That argument, however, is misleading. The truth is that many charter school teachers across the country come from traditional public schools; and the vast majority of charter school teachers across the country hold state teaching licenses, as charter school policies in most states require that charter school teachers have state certification. It is true that some states do permit charter schools to hire some nontraditional teachers. North Carolina is one example, where legislation requires that at least 75% of teachers in charter schools in grades kindergarten through 5 hold valid North Carolina teaching certificates, and that at least 50% of teachers in charter schools in grades 6 through 12 hold valid North Carolina teaching certificates.

Charter school critics have argued against the policy waivers that charter schools receive in many states. Charter schools receive the waivers granting them additional autonomy in exchange for being held to higher levels of performance accountability. Charter schools critics argue that if charter schools are provided waivers from onerous and unnecessary policies and regulations, traditional public schools should be provided with waivers from the same policies. Interestingly, many charter school advocates have agreed with charter school critics that traditional public schools should receive the same waivers that charter schools receive. But just as with charter schools, they argue that traditional public schools should be held to higher standards of performance accountability, facing the possibility of being shut down if they fail to perform according to agreed upon standards. Some states have experimenting with providing policy waivers to traditional public schools. One example is Kentucky.

Kentucky does not have a charter school law. Teachers unions and Democratic legislators have been very successful with keeping charter schools out of the state. During the 2012 session of the state general assembly, lawmakers passed a *charter-like* bill that allows local school districts to apply for waivers from state regulations through a process very similar to the processes in other states for approving charters. The law is intended to allow traditional public schools to apply for waivers from some regulations so that they may try innovative approaches to teaching and learning. The new Kentucky law will not, however, hold such schools to higher, charter-like standards of performance accountability.

Finally, one of the most frequent criticisms of charter schools has been that they result in the resegregation of public schools. That claim is not true. School segregation is the separation of students in schools according to their race. Charter schools, however, are schools of choice. Parents choose charter schools for their children. No one assigns students to charter schools. The only way a student attends a charter school is if his or her parents apply for admission to that school. And if at some point a parent becomes dissatisfied with the charter school, that parent may disenroll their child at any time and send him or her to another public school. It is true that with parent choice, many parents have chosen to send their children to schools that are more racially isolated than the schools they previously attended (Lewis & Danzig, 2010); in many cases, these have been African Americans who have chosen to send their children to predominantly or all-Black charter schools. So it is accurate to say that an outcome of charter school policy has been the creation of some racially isolated public schools. But to be very clear, parents are making those school choices, which is not the same at all as schools or school districts segregating students by race. Further consideration of the politics of choice, desegregation, and busing is provided in chapter 5.

Final Thoughts

Charter school critics have argued that instead of creating charter schools as additional options for parents, education reform efforts should be limited to improving traditional public schools. That argument, however, is shortsighted. It fails to recognize the reality of the time that we now live in, the futures we must prepare our children for, the demands of the American and global economies for greater levels of expertise and specialization, the increased demands of parents for additional school options, and the complete dysfunctionality of some of our nation's traditional public school districts and schools. The current reality is that our one-stop shop, mass-manufacturing model of public schooling is broken. It has never worked well for some children, and it now serves even fewer children well. Some traditional public school districts and schools can be fixed or revamped, but others cannot; those districts and schools that are beyond repair should be forced to close their doors forever. Those schools serve no one well, and we waste valuable time, scarce resources, and precious lives as we tinker with schools and systems that should have been dismantled long ago. In their place, we should be working together to create more specialized schools of choice for children that will prepare them to live and compete in this ever-changing society and economy. Those schools are what parents in the twenty-first century are demanding for their children.

4

The Politics of Charter Schools and Choice in North Carolina

Charter school legislation was passed by the North Carolina General Assembly and signed by the governor in 1996, with the state's first charter school opening during the 1997–1998 school year. The legislation's passage, however, seemingly came not as a result of a singularly focused effort to bring charter schools to the state. Instead, the passage of charter school policy in North Carolina was a compromise measure. Republican state Sen. Steve Wood, a sponsor of the successful charter school bill, characterized the legislation as a "carrot offered along with the stick of a tuition tax credit bill" (McNiff & Hassel, 2002, p. 210). Parent choice advocates in North Carolina had effectively placed the traditional public education establishment between a rock and a hard place by threatening to continue to press for tuition tax credits and vouchers for private schools if charter schools were not accepted as an alternative measure. In the end, charter school legislation in North Carolina was pretty widely supported by opponents of school vouchers and tax credits as a compromise that would hopefully hold off the stick (McNiff & Hassel, 2002).

North Carolina's initial charter school law had many of the elements recommended by national charter school advocates such as the Center for Education Reform, including (a) permitting individuals or groups to apply for charters, (b) creating multiple charter authorizers with the State Board of Education in place for final approval, (c) allowing charter schools to operate as independent nonprofit corporations, acting as their own employers, (d) automatically exempting charter schools from several state regulations, (e) allowing charter schools to receive operating funding at the same level as traditional public schools, (f) subjecting charter schools to the same testing requirements as district public schools, and (g) requiring charter schools to develop transportation plans so that transportation would not prohibit any student in the host district from attending the charter school. But contrary to the recommendations and desires of state and national choice advocates, North Carolina's law included a provision that capped the number of charter schools that could be authorized at one hundred schools, and provided that no more than five charter schools could be authorized within a school district per year.

Choice advocates temporarily enjoyed the milestone of having passed the state's most significant choice legislation to date, but as early as 2001, they began lobbying in support of raising or removing the charter school cap on the grounds that it limited opportunities for the success of the charter school movement (Kakadelis, 2002). A policy report from the John Locke Foundation, a North Carolina–based conservative policy think tank, asserted that the demand for charter schools in North Carolina was much greater than one hundred schools could accommodate (Stoops, 2007). The report stated that during the 2007–2008 academic year, over 5,200 students were placed on waiting lists for charter schools in North Carolina. Raleigh Charter High School, for instance, received 705 applications for 79 open slots; Franklin Academy Charter School in Wake Forest received 1,524 applications for 101 slots; and Pine Lake Preparatory Charter School in Mooresville received 2,500 applications for 1,200 available slots (Stoops, 2007).

North Carolina parent choice advocates also argued that the general public was supportive of lifting the statutory cap on charter schools. The John W. Pope Civitas Institute (2008), a conservative research and public policy organization, reported that in a January 2008 statewide telephone survey, 47% of respondents indicated that they were in favor of raising the cap of one hundred charter schools and allowing charter schools to operate with fewer restrictions (John W. Pope Civitas Institute, 2008). A 2006 survey indicated that 59% of North Carolinians wanted to see the cap of one hundred charters schools removed, and 52% of North Carolinians said that they were more likely to support a candidate for political office if he or she supported legislation to lift the charter school cap (John W. Pope Civitas Institute, 2008). Also in 2006, A *News & Observer*/WRAL poll showed that 59% of Wake County respondents favored increasing the number of charter schools or offering vouchers to parents whose children attend private schools (Stoops, 2007).

Until the cap's eventual removal in 2011, there had been quite a few unsuccessful legislative attempts to lift or completely remove the state's cap on charter schools, showing that traditional public school interests did not merely fade away and allow charter school advocates to dictate a new status quo after the passage of charter legislation in 1996. Not even the enticement of *Race to the Top* federal funding would be enough to move Democrat legislators to betray their traditional public school advocate friends by supporting legislation to raise or remove the state's charter school cap. But Republican's taking control of both chambers of state general assembly in 2011 would be the end of the cap. Further, the 2012 election of the state's first Republican governor since 1984 signal that the expansion of parent choice policy in North Carolina is on the horizon.

The politics of choice policy in North Carolina, until recently, had been primarily the politics of charter school policy. This chapter provides analysis of the politics surrounding parents' push to expand parental choice in North Carolina and strengthen the state's charter school policy from 1996 until 2011 when the charter school cap was removed by the state legislature. The chapter begins with discussion of advocacy for charter school policy change in North Carolina, divided into the five primary areas that advocacy occurred from 1996–2008: (a) the statutory cap of 100 charter schools, (b) oversight and regulation of charter schools, (c) facilities and funding for charter schools, (d) charter school admissions, (e) the certification of charter school teachers, and (f) charter school teachers' participation in the state teachers' retirement system. Next is a discussion of the politics of advocacy for and opposition to charter school expansion in North Carolina. The chapter concludes with considerations for the future of choice policy in North Carolina.

Charter School Cap

North Carolina's charter school law, when passed in 1996, stipulated that the State Board of Education could authorize no more than one hundred charter schools statewide and no more than five charter schools per year in one local school district. Beginning as early as 1999, charter school advocates started applying pressure in the general assembly to raise or remove the cap, arguing that it was an unnecessary obstacle to the growth of the charter school movement in North Carolina (Hardee, 1999). For much 1999 until the eventual lifting of the cap in 2011, charter school advocates devoted a disproportionate degree of their political energies to fighting to raise or remove the cap.

The most fervent charter school advocates argued that any limit on charter schools whatsoever, even a limit much higher than one hundred, would still be restrictive. Roger Gerber, founder and president of the League of Charter Schools, argued that North Carolina should have no cap and "free the children" (Buchanan & Dyer, 2001, p. A1). Liz Morey, vice president of the League of Charter Schools said, "We're going to have to work really hard to get the cap lifted. There's no reason to have one" (Silberman, 1999, p. B1). Republican representative and gubernatorial candidate Leo Daughtry asserted, "It's been long enough now that we've been able to put the charters under the microscope. Of the charters that are already out there, they have been well received. I think there will be more serious effort to remove the cap now that it will have been reached" (Silberman, 1999, p. B1).

Traditional public school interests, however, strongly opposed charter school advocates' efforts to raise or remove the charter school cap. Traditional public school interests, including groups representing traditional public school employees and state education institutions (i.e., State Board of Education, Department of Public Instruction, local boards of education), felt threatened by potential expansion of charter schools. Traditional public school interests felt threatened because: (a) funding follows students who leave traditional public schools to attend charter schools; (b) all charter school teachers are not required to hold valid North Carolina teacher certification, which teachers groups assert threatens the livelihood of licensed professional educators; and (c) the very concept of charter schools threatens to upend a system that has become entrenched and has enjoyed a virtual monopoly on public education. Traditional public school interests also argued that raising or removing the charter school cap would be premature given the sporadic performance of charter schools. Having no limit on charters, they reasoned, could result in taking too many students and too much funding from traditional public schools, leaving traditional public schools in dire financial straits (Munn, 2001).

By 2001, there were one hundred charter schools in the state. With the statutory cap in place, the State Board of Education was unable to approve any new charters for the 2001–2002 academic year. The Charter School Advisory Committee recommended to the general assembly that the cap not be removed until the release of a report later in 2001 that would assess how the existing charter schools had performed. A spokesman for Democratic governor Mike Easley commented, "[The governor] continues to question the wisdom of a general lifting of the cap without a full review. We need to look at the successes and the failures and figure what the best avenue would be." While the State Board of Education officially held the position that the General Assembly should wait until the release of the report before deciding whether to lift or remove the cap, Phil Kirk, chairman of the State Board of Education, proposed permitting 28 new charter schools for the 2001–2002 academic year—the average number of charters approved in previous years (Buchanan & Dyer, 2001).

The report assessing the progress of existing charter schools, conducted by two independent education consultants, was released in October 2001. It concluded that charter schools had neither hurt nor helped traditional public schools. Following the release of the report, the Charter School Advisory Committee recommended raising the cap by 10% per year (Buchanan, 2002). Disagreement remained, however, among members of the State Board of Education about whether the cap should be lifted. State Board of Education member Wayne Devitt accepted the recommendation of the Charter School Advisory Committee saying that even with lifting the cap the State Board of Education remains in control of the growth of charter schools through the approval and renewal process (Buchanan, 2002). Other members of the State Board believed that the Department of Public Instruction's Office of Charter Schools was already underfunded and understaffed, and that before removing the cap additional funds should be allocated to that office. Another member of the State Board proposed that traditional public schools that lose students to charter schools should be partially reimbursed for the loss of state revenue (Buchanan, 2002). Finally in January 2002, the State Board came to consensus on the issue, and voted to recommend that the General Assembly increase the charter school cap by ten (Johnson, 2002).

During the 2001–2002 session of the general assembly, lawmakers introduced several unsuccessful bills that would have raised or removed the charter school cap. Senate Bill 867, sponsored by Democratic Sen. Wib Gulley, would have reduced the number of charter schools the State Board could authorize in one school district from 5 to 3, and raised the limit on the number of charter schools that could be authorized statewide from 100 to 135. Both House Bill 25 sponsored by Republican Rep. John Blust and House Bill 29 sponsored by Republican Rep. Leo Daughtry, would have completely eliminated the cap on the number of charter schools that could be authorized statewide.

The release of a report in July 2002 from the North Carolina Center for Public Policy Research (NCCPPR), a nonpartisan nonprofit organization, generated a great deal of controversy surrounding the question of whether the charter school cap should be raised or removed (Charter schools, 2002). NCCPPR found three major problems in their study of charter schools. First, charter school students did not perform as well as their traditional public school counterparts on state standardized tests. Second, the center found considerable problems with the racial imbalance of charter school enrollments. Third, NCCPPR discovered that a number of charter schools experienced significant problems with finances and financial record keeping (Vaden, 2002). In closing, the report advised the General Assembly to hold off on raising or removing the charter cap until charter schools were able to meet goals that officials had set for them, including improving academic achievement levels for low-performing or at risk students, and developing innovative teaching strategies (Charter schools, 2002).

During the 2003–2004 and 2005–2006 sessions, legislators introduced several bills proposing raising or removing the charter school cap; again, all were unsuccessful. In 2003, both House Bill 31 sponsored by Republican Rep. Cary Allred and Senate Bill 359 sponsored by Democratic Sen. Linda Garrou would have implemented the recommendation of the State Board of Education and raised the cap from 100 to 110 charter schools that could be authorized statewide. In 2005, Republican Sen. Eddie Goodall sponsored Senate Bill 213 that would have completely removed the cap on the number of charter schools that could be authorized statewide, and Democratic Sen. Larry Shaw sponsored Senate Bill 490 that would have permitted the State Board of Education to authorize up to ten additional charter schools each year.

In June 2007, the NCCPPR released a second report on the progress of charter schools in North Carolina. Again, the center recommended that the cap on charter schools should remain until student performance improves and charter schools are more racially integrated. In an interview following the release of that report, Ran Coble, director of the NCCPPR said, "Charter schools are an important experiment, but just providing a choice is not enough. It's got to be a good choice for educating North Carolina's students. Charter schools need to perform well before we expand the experiment" (Report: Keep charter school cap, 2007, p. B1).

Subsequent to the dissemination of the NCCPPR's second report, during the 2007–2008 session of the General Assembly, legislators introduced several additional unsuccessful bills to raise or remove the charter school cap. Republican Sen. Fred Smith sponsored Senate Bill 39 that would have raised the number of charter schools that could authorized statewide from 100 to 125. Democratic Sen. Doug Berger sponsored Senate Bill 590 that would have permitted the State Board of Education to authorize an additional 25 charter schools "if at least thirty percent (30%) of the students at those schools qualify for free or reduced-price lunches" (lines 19–21); and Republican Reps. David Lewis, Ric Killian, and Curtis Blackwood sponsored House Bill 1638 that would have allowed the State Board during one calendar year to authorize no more than 10% of the previous year's number of operating charter schools statewide.

In June 2007, the State Board appointed a Blue Ribbon Commission on Charter Schools composed of sixteen members, including state legislators, city council members, higher education officials, traditional public school and charter school administrators, business and community leaders, charter school board members, and charter school students. The commission met monthly from June through November, with a four part charge: (a) evaluating the status of charter schools including legislation and policy, (b) determining areas of improvement for charter schools, (c) determining whether current charter school legislation should be adjusted, and (d) determining whether State Board of Education policies should be adjusted or rewritten (Blue Ribbon Commission on Charter Schools, 2008, p. 2). In the end, the commission recommended increasing the charter school cap by six schools per year, and excluding high-performing charter schools from counting toward the cap. Additionally, the commission recommended that the first charter schools in a county that currently does not have one should not count toward the cap (Blue Ribbon Commission on Charter Schools, 2008).

The commission's recommendations were based in part on the belief of several commission members that a complete removal of the cap would have virtually assured that their recommendations would go nowhere. Responses to the Blue Ribbon Commission's recommendations were mixed. Some responses were fairly positive. Tom Humble, Blue Ribbon Commission member and Raleigh Charter High School principal said, "This is a compromise, and it opens up room for more charter schools" (Epps, 2007, p. B5). Terry Stoops, education policy analyst for the John Locke Foundation, said the commission's recommendations were positive and would address the state's demand for charter schools (Epps, 2007). Jack Moyer, director of the Office of Charter Schools in the Department of Public Instruction, also spoke positively about the recommendations (Epps, 2007). Other stakeholders, however, were somewhat disappointed with the recommendations. Businessman and Franklin Academy Charter founder Bob Luddy asserted, "We shouldn't try to second guess what they're [General Assembly] thinking. I was in favor of a much bolder move" (Epps, 2007, p. B5).

Oversight and Regulation

North Carolina's initial charter school legislation established the basic framework for charter schools' application processes, authorization, and accountability system. The specifics of charter school oversight and regulation, however, were left relatively vague. Disagreement between charter school advocates and critics resulted from the legislation's ambiguity. Amendments to the state's charter school legislation, as well as formal and informal policies of the Charter School Advisory

Committee and the State Board of Education, produced a charter school regulatory system that is much less ambiguous. However, disagreement remained regarding the appropriate degree of oversight for charter schools.

North Carolina's charter school law specified what persons or groups of persons were eligible to apply for charters. The law established that any person, group of persons, or nonprofit corporation can apply to start a charter school on behalf of a private nonprofit corporation. It also permitted the conversion of traditional public schools into charter schools, provided that the application included a statement signed by a majority of the school's teachers and instructional support, and evidence that a majority of the school's parents favor conversion of the school into a charter school. Three chartering entities were authorized to grant preliminary approval of applications: (a) local boards of education where the schools are to reside, (b) boards of trustees of constituent institutions of The University of North Carolina, and (c) the State Board of Education. It also allowed charter applicants who had been rejected by chartering entities other than the State Board of Education to appeal to the State Board. The State Board of Education was established as the only entity with the authority to grant final approval to charter school applications. Charter advocates, who see the State Board of Education as a part of the traditional public school establishment and averse to the needs of charter schools, have frowned upon the general assembly's decision to give this sole authority to the State Board. One choice advocate and policy actor related that the State Board of Education had indeed lobbied against the passage of the state's charter school legislation, and that giving the State Board of Education that kind of control over the formation of charter schools was like "leaving the wolves in charge of the sheep."

Second, North Carolina's charter school legislation gave parameters for how charter schools would ultimately be held accountable for fulfilling the terms of their charters. The law stipulated that charter schools are exempt from statutes and rules applicable to local school boards, but that they would be held accountable to the local school district where it resides to ensure compliance with applicable laws and provisions of its charter. Charter schools were to be subject to financial audits, audit procedures, and audit requirements of the State Board of Education. Additionally, the legislation specified that the State Board of Education could terminate or not renew a charter schools' contract for any of the following reasons: (a) failure to meet student performance requirement detailed in the charter, (b) failure to meet standards of fiscal management, (c) legal violations, (d) violation of any standards and procedures set forth in the charter, (e) a request of two-thirds of the faculty and instructional support personnel at the school that the contract be terminated or not renewed, or (f) any good cause. Again, leaving charter schools under the charge of the traditional public school establishment, or what one interest group representative referred to as the "BLOB—Big Learning Organizations Bureaucracy," was from the very beginning an area of discontentment for charter school advocates.

Next, charter school legislation authorized the State Board of Education to establish the Charter School Advisory Committee, a group that would play a significant role in the application, authorization, and oversight of charter schools. The Charter Schools Act stated that the committee's responsibilities were to include providing technical assistance to chartering entities or to potential applicants, reviewing charter applications for preliminary approval, making recommendations on charter approval termination and nonrenewal to the State Board of Education, and making recommendations to the State Board regarding grievances between charter schools and their chartering entities.

Traditional public school interests won a significant early battle related to charter school oversight policy. Specifically, with the Amend Charter School Laws Act passed in 1997, charter applicants seeking preliminary approval from the State Board of Education or a University of North Carolina constituent institution were required to also submit a copy of the application to the local school district where the proposed charter school would reside. The local school district could submit its comments concerning the application to the chartering entity where preliminary approval is sought. Charter school advocates saw this change in policy as a victory for traditional public school interests seeking to stymie the formation of new charter schools. The amendment, however, did not stipulate that local school districts must give approval to proposed charter schools. Nevertheless, charter school advocates asserted that requiring the involvement of local school districts in the application process of all charter schools was, as one interest group put it, "just one more step backwards for charter schools."

Charter schools' required participation in the state's academic accountability and testing program was a second triumph for traditional public school interests. North Carolina's basic school accountability system, called the ABCs of Public Education, uses end-of-grade tests in elementary and middle school and end-of-course tests in high school to measure students' progress from year to year. Charter advocates cite the requirement that charter schools administer the state standardized exams as a case in point that traditional public school interests are successfully pushing charter schools away from the model of an alternative to traditional public schools and forcing them to look more and more like traditional public schools.

Initially, groups applying for charters had the option of deciding indicating in the charter application whether they would participate in the state's testing program. For example, during the 1997–1998 academic year, the first year of operation for charter schools in North Carolina, School in the Community Charter School gave only 12 of its 77 students end-of-grade tests. Leaders of the school justified their decision to administer the test to a select group of students saying, "For many of our kids, the primary goal is getting them interested in learning again. Many of our students did relevant work, but it wasn't material that the state tests for on the ABC exams" (Charter schools need to meet benchmarks, 1998). The change to require all charter schools to participate in North Carolina's ABCs, however, was made very early on. In fact, according to one interest group representative, charter schools' right to opt out of state testing was taken away after the publication of a *News & Observer* article reporting School in the Community's minimal participation in state testing. He recalled:

> That was in the paper and it all happened in front of the general assembly. The House read the paper and everybody stood up and said let's mandate the test. So everyone was mandated to take the test. So we're all mandated to take the state test.

The testing requirement for charter schools has been and continues to be a very contentious issue for charter school advocates. Results of state tests for a number of charter schools have not been very promising, and some charter school advocates have loudly questioned their mandatory participation in the state's testing program. Charter school advocates have argued that state tests prevent charter schools from operating with the flexibility that was promised to them. Tom Williams, principal of Healthy Start Academy in Durham, argued:

> We believe the ABCs are a noble effort to hold schools accountable, but it is a flawed effort.... We are supposed to be creative and innovative. We are supposed to be able to teach Rudyard Kipling rather than Judy Blum. But if we do that, we now see that our test scores will suffer. (Simmons, 1999, p. B1)

Additionally, charter school advocates alleged that the state tests fail to provide teachers and administrators with academic feedback of any value. One charter school official said of the tests:

> I wish we could throw away the state tests because I really feel they're useless. They provide me with no information in terms of trying to construct curriculum to assess student needs. We independently administer the Iowa Test of Basic Skills. It's a nationally-normed test. It allows us to compare ourselves to other schools and students across the entire nation, and gives a much better feeling for how students are performing in subgroups and subcategories. Not just by ethnic or gender or anything like that, but also within a student, are they weak in spelling or is it math computation.

Similarly, one state official's perception of the usefulness of the state standardized assessments was:

> The North Carolina tests basically tell you nothing. They're not diagnostic. Their levels of achievement are very questionable when you compare it to the levels of the NAEP [National Assessment of Educational Progress] test. And the percent of children at different levels is just totally inconsistent with what the NAEP testing tells you with percentages of children. So many charter schools would rather not take the state test, but by law they have to so they do the state test but then they usually give another type of achievement test that is more diagnostic and they can learn more from.

Surprisingly, however, even with charter school advocates' vocal opposition to the state testing requirement, they devoted little, if any, political activism toward changing that requirement. Most study participants reported that this lack of political effort is for two reasons. First, nearly all the political resources of choice advocates in the state had been targeted to efforts to raise or remove the charter school cap; and second, charter school organizers and advocates did not believe that a fight to change the testing requirement could be won. One choice advocate and policy insider said:

> It's not worth the wrath that comes from DPI [Department of Public Instruction] to pick up issues like that. If you pick up an issue and try to fight it, DPI will come down hard on you and you have to pick and choose your fights. And that was a fight that the charter schools said at the very beginning, we'll give the test, no big deal.

Facilities and Funding

Few charter school policy issues received more attention from 1996 to 2008 than charter schools' challenges with securing and paying for school facilities. North Carolinas' charter school legislation stipulated that charter schools could lease space from local boards of education or from public or private nonsectarian organizations. The law prohibited charter schools from using funds allocated by the state to purchase land or buildings, and allowed charter schools to only own land and buildings they obtained through non-state funding sources.

In 1997, amendments to those provisions of the legislation were made with the Amend Charter School Laws Act. Those amendments included provisions allowing charter schools to lease space from sectarian organizations, providing that no religious artifacts were visible. Additionally, the amendments compel local school districts to consider leasing buildings to charter schools. Local boards of education of the local school administrative units where charter schools are located are directed to lease any available building or land to charter schools. Only local boards that demonstrate that leasing facilities is not economically or practically feasible or that the local board does not have adequate classroom space to meet its enrollment needs are permitted to refuse facilities to charter schools. Additionally, the amendments made provision for new charter schools unable to find adequate facilities in the local school district where the school was approved to operate. The amendment allowed the State Board of Education to authorize a charter school to operate within a neighboring county for a one-year period. Subsequent to that one-year period, the charter school would be required to reapply for a charter and receive final approval from the State Board of Education to continue operating in that county.

Still, charter schools found it extraordinarily difficult to find suitable facilities to hold classes. Both interviews and document analysis show that obtaining building space was one of the most difficult hurdles for start-up charters in the state to overcome. Several charter schools had to delay their opening after unsuccessful attempts to find suitable building space, and some charter schools were being housed in places such as old houses, abandoned churches, strip shopping centers, and industrial steel buildings (Price, 1998). Republican state Rep. Fern Shubert commented, "Charter schools have a real handicap. They have to provide a building without having the ability to get a bond referendum passed. How can they be expected to open their doors without some money for a building?" (Lyttle, 1998, p. B5).

Study participants familiar with the plight of charter school organizers attempting to obtain adequate school facilities recounted some of their struggles. One choice advocate shared:

> Since the beginning of charter schools, we've had 40 charters that have gone out. Ten of them have never opened their doors. And most of those were for building reasons. They just couldn't find a building. We've had 30

that closed their doors and some of the problems that they had have basically been around buildings.

Likewise, another choice advocate commented:

> In the very beginning if you went to go to a bank or even a landlord and said, we're opening a public school, we're going to get funded. We're a nonprofit, can we rent your building? They'd look at you and say, are you crazy? It just wasn't happening.

The fact that charter schools do not receive any funding for facilities is tied to the politics of the passage of charter school legislation in 1996. Part of the argument that choice advocates used in North Carolina and around the country was that charter schools are able to do a better job of educating students than traditional public schools, and they can do it with less money. In North Carolina, the less money part of the argument was put into legislation with charter schools receiving only the state and local operating expenses of traditional public schools. Charter schools do not receive the local funds that traditional public schools receive to build school facilities, leaving charter schools to pay for school facilities out of their operating funds.

But even with charter schools receiving fewer total dollars per pupil, some local school district officials have criticized charter schools because funding follows students who leave local school districts to attend charter schools. Local school district leaders have alleged that charter schools "attack" traditional public school revenue sources such as fines and forfeitures, arguing that charter schools are "nickeling and diming" them to death.

Local school district leaders believe that charter schools are a threat to their funding, which has in some cases led to strained relationships between charter schools and local school districts. Nowhere has this tension been manifested more visibly than in the transfer of funds between local districts and charter schools. While some charter schools report having amicable relationships with school districts for the transference of funds, others have had to resort to litigation to get funding to which they are legally entitled. One choice advocate told of the struggle one charter school had with obtaining its operating funds from the local school district. She recounted:

> The school system just looked at them and said no we're not going to give you your money. And held them off for a year without giving them anything. Poor charter school had to go get an attorney because the school system said, we know what the law says but we're just not going to do it.

Another example is Francine Delaney School, which experienced quite a fight in attempting to retrieve funds from the Asheville City Schools. In 1998, voters in the Asheville City School District approved a supplemental tax for the purpose of improving the operation of the public schools, but the Asheville City School District reasoned that this funding should not be a part of the pool of funds to be allocated to charter schools. According to Special Deputy Attorney General Thomas Ziko, the Asheville City School District was obligated to transfer a share of those tax monies to the charter school. Mr. Ziko wrote:

> It is consistent for the local school system to transfer all monies it has budgeted in the current expense fund pro rata to the charter school. This puts public charter school students on an equal footing with students attending the traditional public schools.

After a series of legal battles, the courts found that the Asheville City Schools had unlawfully kept funds from Francine Delaney School and issued a judgment for the school of over $1 million.

In 2005 four charter schools filed a lawsuit against the Charlotte-Mecklenburg Schools in Mecklenburg County Superior Court alleging that the school district had shortchanged them a total $844,762 over the previous four years. Two things were at issue: (a) the Charlotte-Mecklenburg Schools did not include funds for a prekindergarten program and a $6 million high school challenge grant in the pot of money that is shared with charter schools, and (b) the Charlotte-Mecklenburg Schools measured enrollment in a way that penalized charter schools for attrition during the academic year, but did not do the same for its traditional public schools. The Charlotte-Mecklenburg Schools argued that the county approved funding for the prekindergarten high school programs separate from the overall public education budget, and intended that those funds would go only to specific schools (Helms & Morrill, 2005). Richard Vinroot, lawyer for the charter schools and former mayor of Charlotte commented, "If they get away with this, they'd be smart in the future to have everything a special designation—a high school challenge, a junior high challenge and an elementary challenge" (Helms & Morrill, 2005, p. 2B). In 2006, the court awarded the charter schools $165,000. The charter schools challenged the ruling, however, on the grounds that that they were owed much more, and in 2008 a panel of three appeals judges unanimously sided with them, finding that that school district owed them over $400,000 (Helms, 2008). A study participant commenting on the case said, "They fought every dime a charter school would try to get." And even following the court ruling, the willingness of the school district to fulfill its legal obligation to share funds with charter schools is questionable. A Charlotte-Mecklenburg insider shared:

> In a meeting that was held after that, in public record, the school board went back and said we've got to find a way to make sure that we can hide the money or put it in different pots so that charter schools can't get it.

Beginning as early as 1998, charter school operators began to ask counties where they reside for additional funds for capital expenditures. Boards of county commissioners across the state reported being asked for additional funds for capital expenses. But a written opinion from the Special Deputy Attorney General Thomas Ziko in April 1998 declared that counties do not have the legal authority to allocate funds to charter schools for buildings, and that doing so would be a violation of the law (Price, 1998). Ziko wrote:

> It is well-settled that counties possess only those powers delegated authority as the General Assembly may deem fit to confer upon them.... There is no provision of the Charter School Act that authorizes a board of county commissioners to allocate county monies directly to charter schools, whether for capital needs or for operating expenses.... Thus under well-settled case law, the commissioners lack the authority to allocate funds to charter schools for capital outlay.

Some charter school advocates argued that additional funding for charter schools is essential for competing on a level playing field with traditional public schools. A charter school official noted:

> It means that you are scrambling to get quality teachers. I've been on a couple of schools in Wake County especially when Wake County was growing so much and paying bonuses for teachers it was hard to maintain teachers because we didn't have money to pay the extra $3000 they were giving as signing bonuses. It's hard to tell a 25 year old to pass up a $3000 signing bonus and maybe $3000 more a year.

But not all charter school organizers and advocates feel that charter schools require additional funding to be competitive with traditional public schools. Several study participants insisted that some charter schools do not need additional funding for operating or capital expenditures. In fact, according to these participants, some charter schools take pride in being able to do over and above what traditional public schools do, and with less funding.

A charter school advocate explained, "The financing is not that big a deal to some. They actually think that's positive because it keeps you lean and mean. You're not spending money needlessly." According to a charter school official, some charter schools do not need additional funding because they have been able to cut out a great deal of waste that has become commonplace with traditional public schools. He said:

> There's not a lot of overhead here. There's myself and **** that run the school. Everybody else with the exception of people who may be sitting in the front office, they're teachers. And so, there's no layers of central office staff and groups of people There's none of that going on. There's also just, when you're looking at these buildings, they're nice buildings.... And go look at, I mean there's a new high school right around the corner.... I'll be able to building that school for about 120 dollars per square foot. And you go find out what Wake County, Johnston County, any of the ones around here and find out what it is and they're going to say 180, 200, 210. It's just waste. I don't need any more money per pupil. I can operate this school with what I'm getting. I don't need any more.

A state education policy actor expressed concern that asking the general assembly or counties to allocate capital funds to charter schools would diminish some of the argument for charter schools. She explained:

> I support that policy as it is now and it's a simple reason. If we were to fund the building of charter schools we would lose an argument for having more of them. Part of the argument is it saves tax payers money. They're not having to build this building. They have to find their own building. They have to do it with less money. They're not treated the same but in this political dynamic that ought to stay the way it is now for now.

Since 1998, many bills backed by charter school advocacy groups have been introduced proposing additional funding for charter schools.

Democratic Senator Wib Gulley sponsored two unsuccessful bills during the 1997–1998 session, House Bill 274 and House Bill 1386. These bills would have appropriated up to $2 million to the State Board of Education to be awarded to approved charter schools for the 1998–1999 academic year for costs related to start-up. During the 2003–2004 session, the unsuccessful House Bill 1770 would have created a fund to be used by the State Board of Education to match federal funds received by the state under the State Charter School Facilities Incentives Grant Program. The restrictions on state funds allocated to charter schools would not have applied to state funds used to match federal funds received under this grant program.

Additionally, a great deal of controversy has surrounded whether charter schools would receive a share of funding from the North Carolina Education Lottery. The lottery law designates four areas for lottery funds: college scholarships for needy students, aiding local school districts with school construction, prekindergarten programs throughout the state, and reducing class size. The law does not, however, specifically mention charter schools. So while charter schools legally qualify for funds for lower class sizes and their graduates will be eligible for college scholarship funds, they do not qualify for capital funds. Numerous unsuccessful bills were sponsored during the 2005–2006 and 2007–2007 sessions of the general assembly that would have authorized lottery revenue for school construction to flow to charter schools. Each bill died in committee, never even making it to a vote.

Charter school advocates contend that the omission of charter schools from lottery legislation was merely an oversight and not intentional. Others, however, argue that not including charter schools in the lottery bill was not an oversight at all. Democratic state Sen. Kay Hagan asserted:

> It appears to me that most of the areas where the lottery money will be going wouldn't be applicable to charter schools.... There's only 100 public charter schools in the state. Right now, we're really looking at the other 2,000 schools. (Binker, 2006, p. B1)

Charter school advocates argue that the failure of the general assembly to include charter schools in the lottery bill is evidence of the overall treatment of charter schools as second class schools. According to Mary Lou Nance, chair of the board of a Greensboro charter schools, "If we are going to have a lottery and that lottery is going to be used to fund education, then we ought to be fair" (Binker, 2006, p. B1). Similarly, a charter school official commented:

> We're public schools. Why are we not included? That makes no sense to me that you take just 3% of the students who don't qualify for this that was promised in the public funding North Carolina educational lottery. Well, there's no North Carolina education lottery for charter schools.

Similarly, an interest group representative said:

> When you hear the ads education lottery you're a second class citizen if you're a charter school and that 250 dollars per child per year approximately. That adds up if you're on a tight budget. That's still some extra money you can spend on books, or teachers, or rent.

Admissions

As charter schools in North Carolina and across the country are public schools, they are free and open to the public. Charter schools are able to specify in their charters what their unique mission is to be and thus the type of students that they wish to serve (e.g., schools for the gifted, schools for at risk populations, schools for students with special needs). But within those parameters, charter schools, just as other types of public schools, were intended to be open to all students. North Carolina's charter school legislation specifies in no uncertain terms that charter schools are prohibited from discriminating against any student on the basis of intellectual ability, disability, race, creed, gender, national origin, religion, or ancestry.

However, proposed amendments to charter school legislation would have allowed charter schools to give admission preferences to 50% of the former students of a private school converting to a charter school. Concern over any admissions preferences in charter schools was articulated by lobbyists for education interest groups including the North Carolina Association of Educators (NCAE) and the North Carolina School Boards Association, as well as members of the state general assembly. Democratic Sen. Wib Gulley, a primary sponsor of the state's charter school legislation, questioned the proposed admissions preferences saying:

> A fundamental premise of the legislation [original charter school legislation] is charter schools are public schools open to everybody on an equal basis. I think it's going to be very difficult to get the Senate to concur with any system of preferences that differs from public schools. (Rawlins, 1997a, p. A1)

Ben Berlam, a lobbyist for the North Carolina School Boards Association said, "I can't imagine how we can tell the people of North Carolina that because a student wasn't in a private school last year that has converted to a charter school, they can't apply. We could never support preferences" (Rawlins, 1997a, p. A1). Similarly, John Wilson, president of NCAE commented, "Admissions preferences are tantamount to allowing private schools to convert to charter schools" (Rawlins, 1997a, p. A1).

Even with intense debate in the House surrounding the controversial admissions preferences, the proposed legislation with admissions preferences provisions successfully passed in a vote of the House by a 73 to 41 margin (Rawlins, 1997b). Voting fell largely along party lines with 13

Democrats and 60 Republicans voting in favor, and 41 Democrats voting in opposition to the bill (Rawlins, 1997b). One dissenting Democrat, Rep. Bob Hensely argued, "You are using public money to foster a private purpose, using tax dollars to foster schools with admission preferences. It makes some students a little more equal, some parents a little more equal and that is not right" (Rawlins, 1997b, p. A3).

The Senate, however, rejected the House's version of the proposed amendments (Charter school bill faces revamp, 1997). The House and Senate then appointed negotiators to work out differences, and in a compromise bill the House and Senate agreed to giving priority in charter school admissions to siblings of students in the school; children of teachers, teachers' assistants, and principals; and, in the first year, children of members of the school's initial board of directors as long as the prioritized students account for no more than 10% of a school's total enrollment or a total of 20 students, whichever is fewer (Charter schools compromise OK'd, 1997).

Teacher Certification

North Carolina's charter school legislation requires that at least 75% of teachers in charter schools in grades kindergarten through 5 hold valid North Carolina teaching certificates, and that at least 50% of teachers in charter schools in grades 6 through 12 hold valid North Carolina teaching certificates. Since the passage of the state's charter school legislation, the teacher certification requirements of the law have resulted in little debate. Charter school operators have not mounted noticeable opposition to the requirements. But clearly, the fact that not all charter school teachers are required to hold teacher certification has fueled traditional public school interests' hostility toward charter schools.

There was consensus from study participants, both charter school advocates and opponents, that while everyone did not wholeheartedly agree with the teacher certification requirement, most had accepted it as the law. One study participant and charter school advocate said, "It's part of the law. They're supposed to have 75% K through 5 and 50% 6 through 12 certified teachers. That's the law." Additionally, charter school advocates believe that having properly trained teachers is essential to the continued growth of both individual charter schools and the charter school movement in North Carolina. One charter school official noted, "We never were involved in saying that you should be able to get by if you're not certified. If you don't have the requirements then basically it's black and white." Another participant spoke specifically of the importance of charter schools attracting and retaining quality, certified staff:

> Early on people said I don't know if I want to go to a charter school because they can hire just anybody to be a teacher. Just that idea that someone would be teaching their kids that might not have that degree, that certification. And it can be a valid concern. And I think to help legitimize, to give legitimacy to charter schools you have to not open yourself up to that kind of attack. We have to try to seek out quality people.... The only way to compete with the other public schools is to have a real sound footing in what you're doing. And part of that's having qualified people.

While charter school operators and advocates have not openly challenged the teacher certification requirements of the charter school law, several charter schools have struggled to meet the law's requirement. Some participants believed that charter schools' difficulties stemmed from a slow paperwork process at the Department of Public Instruction, and teachers who are licensed in other states and applying for North Carolina certification. Amidst mounting pressure from traditional public school interests to enforce the teacher certification requirement, in April 2008, the State Board of Education passed a new policy that financially penalizes schools that are out of compliance. The new policy allows the State Board of Education to take away the state's share of the salary of the headmaster, and later for teachers until standards for teacher certification are met.

Early opposition to the State Board of Education's new policy has come from charter school operators contending that such a harsh penalty could force some charter schools into closing (Charter schools get new faculty rules, 2008). However, most study participants expressed neither support nor disdain for the new policy.

Teacher Retirement

A battle spanning five years ensued over charter school teachers' eligibility to participate in North Carolina's teacher retirement system. At the root of the issue was the question of whether charter school teachers would be considered state employees, or, since charter schools are operated by boards of directors of nonprofit corporations, would they be seen as private employees of that corporation. The original charter school legislation stipulated that for the purpose of providing state-funded employee benefits, employees of charter schools electing independence from school districts were not deemed employees of the local school district and were not entitled to state-funded employee benefits including membership in the North Carolina Teachers' and State Employees' Retirement System.

Traditional public school interests saw keeping charter school teachers out of the teachers' retirement system as a way to impede the progress of charter schools in recruiting and retaining qualified veteran public school teachers. Immediately, charter school organizers recognized this limitation. An interest group representative recounted:

> The treasurer had ruled that charter schools could not be in the state retirement system which is good and bad. Bad if you're trying to recruit teachers that have 25 years because they want their five more years. They're not going to leave if they can't keep their retirement.

Thus, charter school interests moved into action to push for change in the policy to allow charter school teachers to participate in the state retirement system.

One study participant remembered, however, that one sticking point was with the IRS. He recounted, "The IRS was ruling that you have to be a state employee, so are you a state employee if you're employed by a charter school that's funded by the state but run by a non-profit?" He described the steps taken by charter school advocates:

> We decided we were all going to visit Senator Helms' office to see. We didn't see him but we saw a representative. The representative said this is a local issue, we're not involved in this. One guy was smart enough to say the IRS is the one that's holding it up. Senator Helms was always known to help constituents. Within 12 hours, certainly within 24 hours the IRS was calling the state saying let's see what is required.... The IRS just got on it because Senator Helms had some power to make them jump, and they wanted to make sure he was happy.

Charter school interests celebrated amendments to the original charter school law that changed the eligibility requirements for charter school teachers to participate in the state teachers' retirement system. A provision of the Amend Charter School Laws Act sponsored by Democratic senator Wib Gulley and passed in 1997, declared that all charter school employees were deemed employees of the local school district for purposes of providing state-funded benefits. The General Assembly justified this change in the legislation stating that charter schools are public schools and their employees are public school employees and "teachers" for purposes of membership in the North Carolina Teachers' and State Employees' Retirement System.

However, the change in eligibility requirements for charter school teachers had the potential to be a double-edged sword for charter school operators. In January 1998, Jack Pruitt, director of the North Carolina Retirement Systems Division, sent a memorandum to all charter schools advising them that teachers and other full-time, permanent employees of charter schools were required to enroll in the Teachers' and State Employees' Retirement System by February 1, 1998. The memorandum stated that charter schools were required to contribute 6% of employees' salaries along with an employer contribution of 10.6%. Charter school advocates had won in the sense that their teachers were now eligible for participation in the state retirement system, but they had not fully anticipated the costs to charter schools associated with their participation. Bill Estes, principal of Orange Charter School in Hillsboro, said that cost to his school could be as much as $20,000. A temporary reprieve for charter schools came with an opinion letter from Senior Deputy Attorney General Ann Reed, on January 29, 1998, stating that the Retirement System's interpretation of the charter school law requiring mandatory participation by charter school employees was correct, but that the Retirement System could "reasonably and responsibly delay implementation of mandatory participation until July 1, 1998."

With the news that the new legislative amendments would require charter schools and their teachers to participate in the state retirement system, and the realization that the unforeseen financial burden to charter schools associated with their participation would be substantial, some charter school operators began to experience what one journalist referred to as "buyer's remorse." While many charter schools had lobbied and advocated for the right to participate in the Teacher's State Retirement System, several were deciding that they would rather not participate. One interest group representative recounted, "So we said, can we do it like universities where professors can elect state retirement or can have their own policies. And we got word, no it's all or nothing because if you guys have this choice, regular teachers are going to want this choice."

During the 1997–1998 session of the general assembly, several unsuccessful bills were introduced in the general assembly, including Senate Bill 1551 sponsored by Democratic senator Wib Gulley and House Bill 1739 sponsored by Republican representative Leo Daughtry. These bills would have changed the provision of charter school law requiring mandatory participation in the North Carolina State Retirement System. During the 2001–2002 session, however, a compromise was reached with the Local Flex, regarding Charter School Teachers Act passed in 2001, sponsored by Republican representatives Allred and Ross. This amendment to the charter school law changed the mandatory participation provision requiring participation of charter school teachers in the state retirement system and gave charter school boards of directors the power to elect to become participating employers in the Teachers' and State Employees' Retirement System with the caveat that if a charter school elected to participate in the system, all of its employees must participate. This amendment was viewed by charter school advocates as a significant victory for charter schools.

The Politics of Advocacy and Opposition

Charter schools' parents, employees, and boards of directors served as the primary advocates for charter school expansion and policy change favoring charter schools. The political base of support for charter school advocates has been the state Republican Party. From 1996 to 2008, North Carolina charter schools did not enjoy the support of any high-ranking state officials, or many advocates at all outside of those with direct involvement with charter schools. The John Locke Foundation and the North Carolina Education Alliance are not lobbying organizations, but they have produced a substantial amount of research in support of removing the charter school cap. Outside of conservative Republicans and direct charter school stakeholders, only a few additional organizations including the League of Charter Schools, Americans for Prosperity in North Carolina, and Parents for Educational Freedom in North Carolina (PEFNC) have been active in their support for lifting or removing the charter school cap. These organizations have engaged primarily in lobbying the general assembly and engaging in grassroots mobilization. One charter school advocacy interest group representative described her organization's political strategies saying:

> I lobby representing my grassroots members who are for charter schools and we bring them to the legislature. There are times when we would perhaps do grassroots advocacy campaigns. In other words, put up a radio ad or a TV advertisement. We've definitely done some newspaper ads. Call representatives and tell them to help. But it's all of matter of getting people to contact their legislator, raise the profile of charter schools and show people they're supportive of them.

Another charter school advocacy interest group representative spoke similarly of his organization's activities, explaining:

> It includes mostly mobilizing people to contact their legislators either in person or via telephone or email and pushing legislators to support

removing the cap and support charter friendly legislation. We have charter school day at the general assembly where we hold rallies and bring charter schools, we also try to take the press to charter schools and show them how successful they are. We form partnerships with charter schools, parents, advocates, and a broader base.

Another strategy used by charter school advocates in trying to have the charter school cap removed has been applying pressure on local school boards seeking to pass bond referendums. Charter school advocacy organizations have threatened to fight against the passage of school bonds unless local boards of education agree to support lifting the charter school cap either by passing resolutions or changing their legislative agendas to support lifting the cap. One interest group representative commented on the strategy of fighting against school bond referendums saying:

There will be times when we fight bonds of all types. It will always be something we bring up in a school bond fight is look, ya'll have got to raise all this money and raise taxes to build more schools but if we just had three more charter schools in this county, how much could that save, because they have to go find their own building. We provide millions of dollars for school construction in North Carolina, maybe we won't have to provide so much if we raise the cap on charter schools.

Another interest group representative recounted the experience of fighting a school bond saying, "We fought a $1 million bond referendum. We lost. But one of the things is if you start beating these local school bonds that might help get the cap raised on charters schools."

In 2000, a Wake County citizens' advisory committee that actually assisted in shaping a proposed $500 million school bond issue said to the school board that it would only support the bond vote if the board endorsed the committee's call to lift the state's limit on charter schools (Hui, 2000). Again in 2006, an advertising campaign sponsored by Americans for Prosperity North Carolina, the North Carolina League of Charter Schools, and Imagine Schools was linked to a Wake County School Board $970 million school construction bond referendum (New campaign touts charter schools, 2006). Appealing to citizens weary of additional taxes for the purpose of building schools, the campaign ads touted charter schools as alternatives to traditional public schools that do not require additional funding for school facilities.

Pressure from charter school advocacy organizations on one side and from the North Carolina School Boards Association on the other has at times put local boards of education in precarious positions. The North

Carolina School Boards Association has consistently maintained the position that the general assembly should retain the cap of one hundred charter schools statewide. Further, the North Carolina School Boards Association has made special appeals to local boards of education to not break ranks with other school districts. Leanne Winner, government relations director for the School Boards Association, commented, "We have made it very clear to our local school boards that we need to have one voice on issues" (Hui, 2000, p. A1). But in February 2007, amidst pressure from charter school advocates threatening to derail any proposed school bond referendum and feeling a pinch for space due to astronomical growth, the Wake County School Board broke ranks with the School Boards Association and approved a resolution asking the General Assembly to lift the cap of one hundred on the state's charter schools. One study participant commented on the Wake County School Board's change of position on the charter school cap:

> Wake county was getting a great deal of political pressure to support charter schools from the Republican dominated county commissioners who felt like if there were more charter schools, they wouldn't have to build new public schools. The county commissioners gave a great big push, because our growth is so high that we don't have a place for all of the children.

Overall, the strategy of fighting school bonds resulted in only limited success. In Mecklenburg County, charter school advocates were able to successfully defeat a bond referendum in 2005. But a charter school advocacy interest group representative admitted that overall, the strategy is a weak one and would not lead to the removal of the charter school cap. He admitted, "Do I honestly believe if we got 100 county commissions in all of North Carolina to pass resolutions to support more charter schools that that would suddenly change things. I don't."

Additionally, charter schools used were not afraid to go to the courts. With respect to the State Board of Education's diversity policy, one charter school filed an injunction to prevent the State Board of Education from closing charter schools that did not meet the racial diversity standards set in charter school legislation. And with school finance, when funds for charter schools were being were being withheld by local school districts, several charter schools resorted to filing suit to obtain funds that they were entitled.

Even with these strategies, however, for the most part, the efforts of choice advocacy organizations have been disjointed and largely ineffective. Many study participants, including both charter school advocates and critics, commented on the weaknesses and ineffectiveness of charter school advocacy groups in pushing legislation to remove the charter school cap. And choice advocates were even more critical of their own organizations' advocacy efforts. Choice advocates offered several explanations of why they have been unsuccessful in their attempts to have the charter school cap lifted or removed. First, they confess that the charter school movement in North Carolina is one that has been somewhat fragmented, disorganized, and lacking effective leadership. One study participant speaking about the disjointedness of charter school advocacy in North Carolina commented:

> Is there a movement? That's the question! The movement is, if I want to start a charter school, I write a charter application and I see if there's space for me to open a charter school. That's the movement. Again, it's so fragmented, and it's lead by independent schools [charter schools] and communities across the state. Mostly independent.

Another interest group representative spoke extensively about some of the failures of charter school advocacy organizations saying:

> Charter schools have never been able to lobby effectively in the general assembly. And whether that's because they came about so quickly, and putting together a legislative strategy was not in the top priority of charter schools, mainly it's existing. Just getting a charter together and existing. You don't really have time to think about lobbying. The league of charter schools came about to try to do that. Roger Gerber was the head of that and Roger did a pretty good job. The thing about lobbyists is, you have to have relationships with General Assembly members whether you like it or not. And you have to have relationships with them no matter what their vote is on another issue. Roger has had a real tough time building relationships with people he disagrees with. They're just not that effective.

Charter School Opposition
Policy insiders and advocates pointed to two interrelated organizations as the biggest hurdles for charter school advocates to overcome in their quest to lift or remove the charter school cap: the state Democratic Party and NCAE. Partisanship has undeniably played a significant role in the legislative debate over the charter school cap. Generally, Republicans have tended to favor lifting the cap and Democrats have tended to favor leaving it in place. Because the General Assembly has been dominated by the Democratic Party, choice advocates had a pretty difficult time trying to get legislation passed that would lift or remove the charter school cap. Partisanship figured prominently in the debate over the charter school cap. One state government official conveyed, "Many of the Democrats have

been pretty cool about doing anything. The Republicans are the ones, the conservative Republicans are very adamant about putting charter schools out there." Likewise, an interest group representative commented:

> I think Republicans in general are for charter schools and Democrats in general are against them. What you get out of Democrats in the General Assembly is, "Oh I support more charter schools! I love charter schools!" But they support leaders that they know won't do that. So they are complicit.

Even though the debate was largely a partisan one, support and opposition for lifting or removing the charter school cap was not entirely along party lines. The state's charter school legislation passed in 1996 was passed with bipartisan support. Additionally, document analysis shows that Democratic legislators in the general assembly have sponsored nearly as many bills to lift or remove the charter school cap as Republican lawmakers. Several study participants cautioned against looking at the issue only through partisan lenses. In fact, they advanced that there are increasing numbers of Democratic legislators who support raising the cap on charter school schools. According to one state education insider:

> I think that a lot of opposition comes out of some of the Democratic quarters and it seems like this is kind of a Republican–Democratic, but that's not totally true because there are a lot of Democrats that support charter schools. There are a lot of liberals that don't support charter schools, and a lot more conservatives that do support charter schools. But I think right now it's so fluid that a lot of people are changing attitudes toward charter schools.

Similarly, a state policy actor commented:

> Some of the Democrats are also in favor of it. Earline Parmon, who is the co-chair of the House committee on K-12 education, actually is the principal of a charter school, and she was the main speaker at this press conference on this thing we're going to give you a copy of. Larry Shaw from Fayetteville, an African American Muslim from Fayetteville, is one of the sponsors of legislation to raise the cap. But even though we had a majority of senators in favor of raising the cap, the way the senate works is that you have to have the leadership.

Several statewide organizations, including the North Carolina Association of School Administrators and the North Carolina School Boards Association, have included maintaining the charter school cap of one hundred in their legislative agendas. Additionally, several study participants specifically mentioned these organizations as opponents of raising or removing the charter school cap. But by far, NCAE was the most vocal and arguably most active of the statewide organizations opposing the expansion of charter schools in the state. Both document analysis and interviews show that no organization had nearly the level of influence in political battle over the charter school cap as NCAE. In fact, charter school advocates argued that the most crucial component to understanding why the majority of Democratic lawmakers have not been supportive of efforts to lift or remove the charter school cap is Democratic lawmakers' relationships with NCAE, the largest and most influential professional educators' organization in the state. Study participants said bluntly that NCAE has tremendous influence over many Democratic members of the state General Assembly. One policy actor went so far as to say, "The reality is they [Democrats] won't do anything unless NCAE says so." According to one state education official:

> They're [NCAE] against it and they're very powerful. They donate a lot of money to politicians, Democrats. And they are single handedly, outside of elected officials, they have been the ones that have stopped it. There is nobody else.

Another policy actor commented on the political and financial influence of NCAE:

> Well, NCAE is a very strong political group. It has a membership of several hundred thousand teachers. Now they'd like to say that those teachers will all vote the way they endorse candidates, and that's not true. But the legislature for two reasons will not cross NCAE as a general rule: one because of that perceived voting power, and two because they give a lot of money to candidates during election time. And candidates don't generally cut off pipelines that feed money into their campaign.

Whether the state's cap on charter schools should be lifted was a frequent topic of debate between candidates during the 2008 North Carolina gubernatorial campaign. Republican candidate Pat McCrory, during his unsuccessful bid for the governor's mansion in 2008, favored lifting the cap as part of his overall education plan for bringing more competition in education to North Carolina. McCrory said, "Choice is good in public schools. It's shortsighted to limit expanding the current cap on charter schools when you have a 30% drop-out rate" (Bonner, 2008, p. B1). Richard Munger, the Libertarian candidate, also favored lifting the charter school cap, saying, "Allowing more charters is the first thing I would press for. It's the centerpiece of my education program.... Rich people have choices now. I want everyone to have a choice" (Bonner, 2008, p. B1). Democratic candidate Beverly Perdue, who won the election, was the only major party candidate who did not support lifting the charter school cap. Lt. Governor Perdue argued, "It doesn't make sense to allow more charter schools when some don't do a good job. The goal with the whole charter philosophy is shut down the ones that don't create innovation and change, and keep the stream of newness coming" (Bonner, 2008, p. B1). Several participants tied Governor Perdue's stance on charter schools to NCAE's financial contributions to her and other Democrats' campaigns. An interest group representative remarked:

> The teachers union [NCAE] provides tons of money to campaigns; to Perdue's campaign, to the State Democratic Party, to the Democratic state senate and house committee. It was tons of money. Nothing illegal about it, but it is a pay to play.

Similarly, another participant said succinctly, "NCAE gave a lot of money to Bev Perdue in the last couple of weeks of her campaign. Enough said."

Despite strong opposition from traditional public school interests, study participants were at least confident that charter school policy as it stood was safe, and that even with Democratic control of the legislature and the governor's mansion, legislative action would not be taken or even attempted that would seek to eliminate charter schools. A policy insider commented:

> People might talk about, will the general assembly ever pull the plug on charter schools? And we rent our space out, but there are schools building charter schools, and borrowing money through a lender to do it.... Short answer is I see it as a stable system. It's in place. I don't think it will back track.

Likewise, another study participant commented, "I think the 100 schools is a pretty stable thing. Going forward, I don't see people rolling that back, it is a natural movement, and it would make pretty big waves if they moved that back."

There was near consensus among choice advocates, however, that as long as the general assembly and governor's mansion was Democrat-controlled, the chances of passing legislation to eliminate the charter school cap are very slim. In 2008, their short-term outlook on raising or removing the charter school cap was bleak. Prophetically, one participant said, "It will not go anywhere over there. It will get pushed around. It won't get heard until the makeup of the legislature changes." Another participant lamented:

> It's pretty bleak in North Carolina. A lot of this comes from the fact that the North Carolina Senate has been under one party rule for 138 years and frankly two people run the Senate, the Speaker and the majority leader. Between Basnight and Tony Rand if they don't want something it doesn't happen. And if they want something it probably will happen. And charter schools is not high on their agenda.

In 2009, North Carolina's interest in competing for funds through the Obama administration's "Race to the Top" again brought the state's charter school cap to the forefront of education policy discussion. In order to compete for funds, the contest required that states submit plans for overhauling education systems with specific components, one of which was easing restrictions on charter schools. North Carolina's charter school cap put the state at a decided disadvantage for receiving funding. Again, attempts were made in the legislature to raise and remove the cap, and again, those attempts were unsuccessful. Recognizing that the state's charter school cap could put it out of the running for "Race to the Top" funds, Governor Perdue, the state superintendent of education, and chair of the State Board of Education wrote to US education secretary Arne Duncan, objecting to the program's emphasis on charter schools as a major tool for innovation. Not surprisingly, their letters did not result in any change to the rubric the US Department of Education applied to funding proposals, and North Carolina was unsuccessful in this first round of *Race to the Top* funding.

Advocacy and Opposition (2008–2012)

Since 2008, the political landscape in North Carolina has changed in ways that greatly favor the expansion of choice policy. The 2011–2012 general assembly was the first since 1870 in which Republicans controlled both chambers of the legislature. The tide began to turn for choice advocates rather quickly. In June 2011, Governor Bev Perdue signed a measure into law eliminating the cap on charter schools in North Carolina. As of January 2013, North Carolina had 114 operating charter schools serving approximately 50 thousand students, with 25 new charter schools scheduled to open in August 2013 and over 150 organizations that had submitted letters to the State Board of Education with the intent of applying to open a school in August 2014. Also, with the lifting of the charter school cap, North Carolina is seeing greater interest from national charter management organizations.

For several years, PEFNC had advocated and worked to organize grassroots support for a tax credit bill in North Carolina. As with most parent choice measures in the state, the North Carolina Association of Educators (NCAE) has opposed such a measure, arguing that the state cannot afford it. But an opening for tax credit policy opened during the 2011–2012 legislative session with HB 344, which proposed giving parents of children with special needs a tax credit for private school tuition and therapy expenses. PEFNC president Darrell Allison reasoned that such a measure did not work against traditional public schools but complements them, as "public schools can't always provide all the help a special needs child requires" (Minchin, 2011). House Bill 344 passed both house of the legislature in June 2011 with bipartisan support; over half of the Democrat members of both chambers of the legislature voted in support of the bill. And in July 2011, Governor Perdue signed the Tax Credit for Children with Disabilities Act into law, allowing parents of children with disabilities to claim state tax credits for education expenses. The law allows parents up to $6,000 a year in state tax credits for expenses from private school education and therapy for children with special needs.

PEFNC has continued to push for additional tax credit policy options. The group has lobbied during previous sessions of the general assembly for a law allowing corporations the option of the diverting their state tax dollars to a scholarship funding organization. House Bill 1104 introduced in 2012 and sponsored by both Democrat and Republic members, would have done just that, allowing the scholarship funding organization to then use those dollars to distribute scholarships in amounts up to $4,000 per student per year to be used for private school tuition, fees, books, or other school expenses. To be eligible for scholarships, students would have to come from a family with an income below 225% of the federal poverty level. In 2012, that income requirement would have been about $53,000 per year for a family of four.

In 2012, North Carolina elected its first Republican governor in over 20 years. Governor Pat McCrory is the first Republican to move into the governor's mansion since James Martin left office in 1993, and only the third Republic governor elected in North Carolina since the turn of the twentieth century. McCrory's victory marks the first time since the 1800s that Republicans have had complete control of the executive and legislative branches of state government. McCrory, having previously served a record 14 years as mayor of Charlotte, ran unsuccessfully for governor in 2008, losing narrowly to then lieutenant governor Beverly Perdue. But with extremely low approval ratings, Perdue, who was North Carolina's first female governor, announced early in 2012 that she would not seek reelection, and McCrory cruised to a relatively easy victory in the November 2012 election.

McCrory ran for governor on an education platform that included providing expanded educational choices for North Carolina families and students. McCrory's ideas around expanded choice include expanding high school diploma options for students to include both a college-ready and a separate career-ready diploma option; expanding virtual school and virtual course options for students; and reducing the number of families on charter school waiting lists by implementing a smoother and more efficient process for charter school authorization.

In response to Republican control of state government, a group of nonprofit organizations from across the state have banded together in a new group called Public Schools First NC. According to the group's website, it formed "out of deep concern about the growing threat to privatize and weaken North Carolina's public schools" (Public Schools First NC, 2012). The group opposes efforts to create or expand education savings accounts, vouchers, and tax credits, and supports only "a limited number of truly innovative charter schools designed to work with local school districts, managed with careful local and state oversight" (Public Schools First NC, 2012). The formation of the group is just one indicator of the defensive position that traditional public school advocates in the state have been forced into. With their partners, state Democratic lawmakers, now the minority party in state government, opponents of choice policy expansion are banding together and preparing for the fight of their lives. Choice advocates in North Carolina are extremely hopeful about the expansion of choice policies in the state. PEFNC president Darrell Allison was hopeful in January 2013 that new leadership would mean an even greater potential for expanding choice policy. Allison commented, "You have new leadership that's not averse to other school models playing a greater role in the education of our children.... It's a paradigm shift" (Frank & Bonner, 2013). Expect to hear a lot about choice policy expansion in North Carolina in the coming years.

5

Busing, Desegregation, and Parent Choice

Du Bois's (1935) question of whether Black children should attend racially integrated schools to receive a high-quality education is one that continues to trouble education policy discussion and debate in the United States. Du Bois answered the question by asserting that the quality of education provided by a school was of greater importance than the school's racial composition, and that Negro-only schools were necessary only to the extent that they were needed to provide a quality education to the Negro people. Du Bois's question has continually been debated in the courts, in Congress, in state legislatures, and by local boards of education. Most notably, his question took center stage in the landmark *Brown v. Board of Education* case, with the US Supreme Court ultimately deciding that separate schools for Black and White children are "inherently unequal." While the Court's decision decided for the nation whether government would separate children by race for the purpose of schooling, questions do remain: Should children be able to attend racially separate schools if their parents choose to send them to such? Should government play a role in ensuring that racially separate schooling does not occur, even if it results at the hands of parents' school and housing decisions? And given the competing educational policy goals of parent choice and racial balance, which goal should receive priority in educational policy considerations? Conflicting answers to these questions serve to support divergent directions for education policy relating to public school diversity and parent choice.

After a period of decreased racial isolation in US schools from the late 1960s through the 1970s, racial isolation is again rising (Frankenberg & Lee, 2003). While only approximately 25% of the US population is nonwhite, over 40% of American public school students are nonwhite, with the vast majority of those nonwhite students attending schools that are substantially segregated by race (Orfield & Lee, 2007). Research has shown that the racial composition of schools is highly correlated with both student achievement scores and the presence of highly qualified and experienced teachers (Lee, 2004a). Part of the explanation for these findings is that race and socioeconomic status in the United States are highly correlated. Since Black and Hispanic children are significantly more likely to be poor, racially isolated minority schools are much more likely to be high-poverty schools as well (Rumberger & Palardy, 2002). For example, in a study of Metropolitan Boston, Lee (2004b) found that 97% of the schools that were less than 10% White faced concentrated poverty, while only 1% of schools that were less than 10% students of color faced such high-poverty conditions.

In the years following *Brown* and up to the present, scholars have questioned whether *Brown's* impact on educational equity has been substantive or symbolic, given the reality that large urban school districts including the Atlanta Public Schools and Chicago Public Schools have student populations that are over 90% minority with more than half of their students eligible for free or reduced-price lunches (McNeal, 2009). Research has shown that most racially segregated schools share the characteristics of having relatively lower teacher quality, fewer total years of teaching experience, persistently low student achievement, low graduation rates, and high dropout rates (McNeal, 2009; Orfield & Lee, 2007). Still others question whether the goal of having racially and socioeconomically balanced schools and classrooms should supersede parents' ability to make school choices for their children. This chapter explores some of the most debated issues surrounding the parent choice policies and the racial and socioeconomic balancing of schools.

Charter Schools: Choice and Diversity

An initial claim of some charter school advocates was that charter school reform would result in the reduced racial isolation of students in public schools. They reasoned that giving parents of poor children of color currently trapped in failing racially isolated schools the opportunity to enroll their children in "better," more diverse schools would result in more racially balanced schools and classrooms for all children. By and large, however, this has not occurred. In fact, studies have shown that in some cases charter schools may contribute to children attending more racially isolated schools (Bifulco & Ladd, 2007; Cobb, Glass, & Crocket, 2000; Fuller, Gawlik, Gonzales, & Park, 2003;

Harman, Bingham, & Hood, 2002). Cobb et al. (2000) examined the degree of ethnic/racial stratification in charter schools in Arizona and found that while patterns of racial segregation were not discernible when considering Arizona's charter schools in the aggregate, comparing charter schools to neighboring traditional public schools revealed that approximately one-third of Arizona's charter schools contributed to racial separation during the 1998–1999 school year. Further, their results showed that more Arizona students attended racially segregated schools in 1998 than in 1996. Similarly, comparing the degree of racial isolation in charter schools to traditional public schools in close proximity in 16 states, Frankenberg and Lee (2003) found that charter schools were significantly more racially isolated than their neighboring traditional public schools. Seventy percent of Black charter school students attended intensely segregated schools. Latino charter school students were less segregated than Black charter school students, but they were considerably more segregated than White students. White charter school students in every state attended schools with a disproportionately higher percentage of Whites than the White percentage of the overall charter school population.

In a nationwide study examining inequality and disparities both within charter schools as a group, as well as between charter schools and traditional public schools, Fuller et al. (2003) found that charter schools where more than half the enrollment was African American relied more heavily on teachers who were not licensed. In predominantly African American schools, 60% of teachers worked with an emergency, provisional or probationary certificate, compared to 44% of teachers in predominantly White charter schools. Also, predominantly African American schools were significantly less likely than predominantly White schools to be in compliance with special education laws requiring the development of individualized education programs (IEPs) for students identified as having special needs. Further, Bifulco and Ladd (2007) found that Black students who transferred out of traditional public schools and into racially segregated Black charter schools experienced a much greater negative effect on math achievement than both nonblack students, and Black students who transferred into a nonracially segregated charter school. Findings that charter schools have smaller percentages of traditionally credentialed educators is not surprising given that a goal of the charter school movement has been to bring greater innovation into public schooling, with nontraditional teachers being one of those innovations. In some states, including North Carolina, charter school laws are written specifically to allow nontraditionally credentialed teachers into the classroom. Obviously, debate continues surrounding the correlation of teacher licensure and teacher quality, but findings of noncompliance with special education law and negative effects on student achievement are undeniably concerning, and must be investigated further.

An initial concern of the public and policy makers around charter schools was the possibility that charter schools would become racially isolated havens of refuge for middle-class and affluent White families. As the previously referenced research shows, that has not happened. In fact, what has more often resulted has been parents of color choosing to send their children to more racially isolated charter schools than the district-assigned schools they previously attended. In a study of African American parents' decision-making when choosing a charter school for their children, Lewis and Danzig (2010) found that parents considered a multitude of factors beyond a schools' achievement scores when choosing a school. Parents' reasons for choosing a school included teacher quality and experience, classroom and school size, comfort level with a school and school staff, and the race and gender distribution of teachers and staff. Similarly, some educational leaders have argued that the great numbers of Black children in charter schools, particularly in predominantly Black charter schools, is attributable to the racism that Black families experience in traditional public school systems. Ruth Hopkins, principal of the all-Black Carter G. Woodson Charter School in Winston-Salem, NC, purported that traditional public schools are often characterized by "a culture that holds down expectations, invites excuses and creates failure [for Black students]. The race that is the majority is more enthusiastic about supporting its own" (Associated Press, 1998a, p. 5C). Jeanne Allen, president of The Center for Education Reform, a Washington DC–based charter school advocacy group, voiced similar sentiments saying, "I think what we are seeing is that charter schools attract parents who feel the most disenfranchised from their schools. The South has been plagued with the question of how to educate black children" (Associated Press, 1998a, p. 5C).

Further, Gregory Cizek, education professor at the University of North Carolina at Chapel Hill, is careful to point out that Black parents choosing to send their children to predominantly Black charter schools today is quite different than either the de jure segregation of days past or the de facto segregation of the present. According to Cizek:

> They're choosing it. It's an option for them that they clearly want to pursue. I think it's somewhat different from the old segregation days. People are deciding that it's a better option for them than the school that they would be assigned to. (Vaden, 2002, p. A5)

In 2013, one would be hard-pressed to find a group that would label itself as opposing racial diversity in schools. Instead, the major point of contention around this issue is how highly prioritized racial diversity in schools should be in education policy. Advocates of racial balance in schools have frequently found themselves opposing advocates of parent choice policies who argue that having choices for families should be a greater education policy priority than achieving racial diversity. The values of choice and racial balance have and will continue to conflict. Their conflict is unavoidable. The question that we have to answer is which value should be prioritized in public policy. One North Carolina education policy actor described his thinking about choice and diversity in the context of charter school diversity policy in this way:

> My position is that we shouldn't determine the lives of kids based on desegregation. We should determine the lives of kids based on the quality of their education. So if I end up with an all-black school, I don't really care, if we educate the kids. Because if we educate kids, they can decide how much integration they want. They can decide how much desegregation they need.... I don't think we should try to influence that. I think what we should say is that you're not permitted to turn away a kid who does not fit the demographic you put in the school. In other words, you can have a school that serves white kids, but you better not ever turn away a black kid who tries to get in.

In the best of both worlds, parents would choose schools for their children that meet their learning needs and their choices would result in racially and socioeconomically balanced schools. In some communities that could very well happen, but in many others, it likely will not; so one of these, choice or racial balance, will have to win out. There appears to be agreement that neither discrimination nor the segregation of students by race will be tolerated; neither discrimination nor segregation are at issue here. The question is whether states and boards of education will prioritize choice over racial balance, or vice versa.

Several state legislatures have decided to address the issue of racial balance in charter schools by including diversity provisions in their charter school laws. On one hand, choice is at the very core of the charter school concept, giving parents the ability to choose a school that lines up with their preferences and meets their children's learning needs. On the other hand, achieving racial balance in public schools has been an education policy goal across the United States since *Brown,* and in some parts of the country, prior to that. Choice is about giving parents the responsibility of deciding what school they want their children to attend based on their personal preferences and their children's needs, learning and otherwise. Racial and socioeconomic balancing is about school districts making decisions about where children should attend school based on the desire to have racially and socioeconomically balanced schools. Both goals are laudable, but one must be prioritized over the other.

In an effort to deal with these potentially conflicting goals, 19 states have written guidelines into their charter school legislation pertaining to the racial/ethnic balance of individual charter school enrollments (Frankenberg & Lee, 2003). North Carolina is one of the 19 states with such a provision. North Carolina's charter school law requires that within a calendar year of a charter school opening, its student body must reflect either the racial composition of the population residing within the county where the school is located, or the racial composition of the special population that the school serves residing within the county where the school is located.

North Carolina's charter school racial composition provision drew quite a few questions. One question was whether a charter school with an African-centered curriculum but an open admissions policy that ends up with an entirely Black student body would be legal. Given the provision's intent—preventing the resegregation of public schools in the state—it seemed clear that lawmakers had not anticipated the possibility that minority parents would move their children from relatively desegregated traditional public schools to predominantly minority charter schools. But these early questions proved to be extremely pertinent and in many ways predictive of how charter schools in North Carolina would evolve. By 1998, at least half of North Carolina's charter schools were more than 85% Black and the State Charter School Advisory Committee was considering whether to revoke schools' charters due to racial imbalance.

Many questions loomed: How would the State Board of Education and/or the General Assembly handle charter school racial imbalance? Among members of the Charter School Advisory Committee, there was initially no consensus as to what should be done. One Advisory Committee member who was also superintendent of the Raleigh Catholic Diocese asserted, "What people don't want to see happen is you re-segregate public schools. We want to be sure we're not creating two separate-but-equal schools systems" (Thompson, 1998, p. 3C). Conversely, the chairman of the Advisory Committee commented, "It does not bother me if a charter school has a certain mission that attracts a certain group of people—white, black, Japanese, whatever" (Associated Press, 1998b, p. 6C); "I don't want to be shutting down schools that parents are actively choosing, but not everyone agrees with me. We don't know what we are going to do" (Associated Press, 1998a, p. 5C).

In May 1998, the Charter School Advisory Committee recommended to the State Board of Education that charter schools be exempted from racial diversity standards, prioritizing parental choice over the goal of racial diversity. The committee's recommendation was that each charter school's racial enrollment be examined, and if a school failed the standard but could show that it had attempted to diversify its enrollment, it would be exempt from the integration rules that govern traditional schools. The State Board of Education accepted the recommendation of the Advisory Committee that charter schools should be monitored to ensure that they are as diverse as possible. Disagreement and ambiguity, however, continued to surround the question of how schools would be held accountable to the law's diversity requirement. Additionally, the State Board had yet to answer the important question of whether it would be fair to permit all-Black charter schools to operate, but prohibit all-White charter schools.

In July 1998 the State Board wrote its official Policy on Charter Schools Racial Balance (Policy ID Number: EEO-U-003). The policy required all charter schools to have open admissions procedures and policies. It further stated that charter schools must have student demographic makeups that fall within the range exhibited by the regular, nonmagnet, nonspecial schools in their counties. The racial composition of charter schools that have a mission that targets a specific population must reflect the percentage of the targeted population in the county. Further, the policy directed the Charter School Advisory Committee to investigate any charter school whose racial makeup does not fall into these ranges to determine whether the charter school made a good faith effort for diversity during its enrollment period. As of 20012, most charter schools in North Carolina remained either predominantly White or predominantly Black, but no charter schools had been closed for violating the racial balance requirement of the charter school law.

Busing, Racial Balance, and Choice

Conversations about expanding choice policy typically include consideration of charter schools, private school tuition tax credits, and school vouchers. But policy debates about parent choice and achieving racial and socioeconomic balance in traditional public schools have been more heated and have involved more children than any of the other choice policy debates. Any contemporary discussion of parent choice and race, particularly in an urban school district context, would be incomplete without considering the impact of the Supreme Court's relatively recent ruling in *Parents Involved in Community Schools (PICS) v. Seattle School*

District No. 1, 2007, striking down student assignment plans in Seattle and Louisville (see *Meredith v. Jefferson County Schools Board*, 2006). The central issue in the cases was whether it is permissible for local boards of education to consider race in school assignment plans and decisions. The school districts in both cases had developed assignment plans with the goals of creating and maintain racially integrated schools (McNeal, 2009). In Jefferson County (Louisville, KY), the school system operated under a court-ordered desegregation decree from 1975 to 2000, after a federal court found in 1975 that the board of education maintained a segregated school system despite the US Supreme Court's ruling in *Brown*. In 2001, one year after the federal court found that the board had achieved unitary status and lifted the decree, the Jefferson County School Board adopted a race-conscious student assignment plan intended to maintain the system's integrated schools. The plan included several school options for parents to choose from based on their address, but the plan's primary goal was to ensure that no less than 15% and no more than 50% of any school's enrollment was African American.

In Seattle, in an effort to respond to school segregation resulting from segregated housing patterns, the Seattle Public Schools adopted an open-choice plan student assignment plan for high schools, through which students were asked to rank their preference for schools. The district then used a series of tiebreakers to determine which students would attend the popular, oversubscribed schools. The first tiebreaker gave preference to students with siblings attending the school; the second considered the student's race in relation to the school's student body racial composition; and the third considered the proximity of the student's residence to the school.

With its ruling in PICS, the US Supreme Court struck down the student assignment plans in both Seattle and Jefferson County. The Court found that the plans were in violation of the fourteenth Amendment to the US Constitution, sending the clear message with their ruling that school districts would not be able to legally assign or deny students admission to schools on the basis of their race, regardless of whether the intent of the assignment plan is to achieve racial integration in schools (*Parents Involved in Community Schools (PICS) v. Seattle School District No. 1*, 2007; McNeal, 2009).

Student Assignment and Choice in North Carolina

Although no school districts in North Carolina were named in the PICS decision, North Carolina districts have a colorful history with student assignment policies and school diversity. Both of North Carolina's largest school districts have struggled with the competing policy goals of choice and racial balance. The following sections provide brief accounts of the ongoing challenges of the Wake County Public School System and Charlotte-Mecklenburg Schools to try to balance the two.

Charlotte-Mecklenburg Schools

Charlotte-Mecklenburg Schools (CMS) is the countywide public school district serving metropolitan Charlotte, NC. Charlotte is the largest city in North Carolina and the seventeenth largest city in the United States, with a population of approximately 1.8 million for the Charlotte metropolitan area. Charlotte is the county seat of Mecklenburg County, North Carolina's most populous county with over 944 thousand residents. Charlotte is the second largest financial center in the United States, home to the headquarters of Bank of American and the East Coast operations of Wells Fargo. Charlotte's economy is a diversified one, including finance, insurance, real estate, sports and entertainment, and high-tech industrial development and manufacturing. Charlotte's expanding economy has driven the region's rapid growth and development since the 1980s (Mickelson & Southworth, 2005).

CMS is the second largest school district in the state of North Carolina. During the 2012–2013 academic school year the district enrolled just over 140 thousand students in grades K through 12 in 159 schools, with the following racial/ethnic distribution of students: 42% African American, 32% White, 18% Hispanic, 5% Asian, and 3% American Indian/multiracial. In 2011–2012 CMS served just over 15 thousand students classified as Limited English Proficient, and approximately 53% of the district's students were classified as economically disadvantaged.

From 1971 until 1999 CMS operated in the shadow of the US Supreme Court's decision in *Swann v. Charlotte-Mecklenburg Board of Education*, The Court ordered that every school in the district have an ethnic makeup mirroring the proportions of African Americans and non–African Americans in the school district. In order to achieve the court-order proportions in schools, CMS adopted a mandatory busing policy. CMS's implementation of busing was notably largely accepted by the community, and was heralded as a model for large urban districts desegregating schools through busing (Douglas, 1995; Mickelson, 2001).

During the 1980s, CMS began losing public support for its mandatory busing, largely attributed to rapid immigration into the region from the

Northeast and Midwest. Immigration into the region resulted in growth, but specifically, two population growth trends developed:

> Relocating white middle-class families swelled the county's suburbs, while ethnic minorities—especially Latino and Asian immigrant students—arrived in the urban center of the county. Latinos are the fastest growing segment of the county's population. The black student population has continued to grow in relative and absolute terms. (Mickelson & Southworth, 2005, p. 253)

As a result of declining support for its mandatory busing policy, in 1992, CMS changed its approach and adopted a mandatory choice system that included the use of magnet schools and limited mandatory busing (Mickelson, 2001; Mickelson & Ray, 1994). As a result of the new plan, one-third of CMS schools became either full or partial magnet schools, with each magnet school having a quota for White and African American Students. CMS's stated goals for the new choice system were: meeting the court's requirements of giving all students the opportunity to attend school near their home and dropping the consideration of race and ethnicity in school assignment decisions, improving student achievement, reducing achievement gaps between students of color and White students, maintaining a desegregated schools, and getting community support for the plan (Godwin et al., 2006).

This policy change, however, did not satisfy all parents, particularly White parents, as the policy still included both limited mandatory busing of students and racial quotas for magnet schools that resulted in some White students being denied admission to magnet schools that had reached their White child limit. The result was a lawsuit filed in 1997 by a parent whose White daughter had been denied admission to a magnet school twice because of her race (see *Capacchione v. Charlotte-Mecklenburg Schools*, 57 F. Supp. 2d 228). In the end, the parents were victorious with the court declaring unitary status for CMS (that the system was no longer a dual one, with schools for Blacks and schools for Whites), a ruling that was upheld after appeal and resulted in the end of busing and the end of considering race and ethnicity with individual student assignment in CMS.

CMS developed a new *School Choice* plan implemented in 2002, which divides the district into four transportation zones, with each zone comprised of predominantly White and predominantly African American neighborhoods. Parents may then select their *home school* or any other school in CMS. CMS guarantees that students' whose first choice is their home school will be assigned there. Students not selecting their home school may select up to three schools and participate in a lottery through which spaces are allocated in oversubscribed schools. However, CMS only provides free transportation to schools within students' transportation zone and to magnet schools that serve a student's transportation zone. Students whose parents do not *choose* a school are assigned to their home school.

Wake County Public School System

The Wake County Public School System (WCPSS) is the countywide public school district of metropolitan Raleigh, NC. Raleigh is North Carolina's capital and second largest city, and the county seat of Wake County, North Carolina's second most populous county and the ninth fastest growing county in the United States. The Raleigh-Cary metropolitan area had a 2011 Census estimate of just over 1.1 million residents. Raleigh has been noted recently by numerous sources for its quality of life and business climate, making the city and the region an attractive relocation destination for families. As the capital city, the North Carolina state government is the city's largest employer, followed by WCPSS and North Carolina State University. Healthcare has been a driver of the city's economy. Since 2004, Raleigh has also been home to Duke Energy subsidiary Progress Energy, which prior to its merger with Duke Energy in 2012 was a Fortune 500 company.

WCPSS is North Carolina's largest school district. During the 2012–2013 school year, WCPSS enrolled over 163 thousand students in 169 schools, with 7.5% of students classified as Limited English Proficient and 33.7% of students eligible for free or reduced-price lunch. During the 2011–2012 school year, the district's racial and ethnic distribution of students was as follows: 49.3% White, 24.7% Black or African American, 15% Hispanic or Latino, 6.3% Asian, 4.3% two or more races, 0.4% American Indian or Alaskan Native, and 0.1% Native Hawaiian or Other Pacific Islander.

The current WCPSS district was created with the 1976 merger of the Raleigh City Schools and the Wake County Schools. At the time of the merger, the former Wake County Schools was 23% minority and Raleigh City Schools was 38% minority (McNeal & Oxholm, 2009). The US Office of Civil Rights (OCR) had found the Raleigh City Schools in violation of Title VI of the Civil Rights Act of 1963, threatening continued federal funding for the district. Further, the Raleigh business community was voicing concerns that White flight had so weakened the city district that its schools' poor condition would negatively impact the economic health of the city and the region. A study conducted in 1965 by researchers from Vanderbilt University concluded that a merger of the city and county districts made fiscal sense, would help the region to develop into major urban economic engine for North Carolina, and would have the effect of stabling racial integration in Wake County. The proposed merger was put on a voter referendum in 1973 and was defeated by a 3–1 margin. The eventual merger in 1976 came as the result of action of the North Carolina General Assembly. An 11% decline in the city's population between 1968 and 1976, a weakening tax base, and noticeable White flight from Raleigh caused great concern for a Wake County residents who recognized that the county's fate was tied to that of Raleigh (Grant, 2009). After the merger, the new board resolved to desegregate its schools, and maintain a racial balance of 15–45% minority students in each school. The board accomplished balancing by redrawing its school attendance boundaries, taking into account factors including the racial composition of neighborhoods, the location of schools, and transportation patterns. As a result of the district's successful implementation of the desegregation plan, the civil rights violations were resolved and the district was declared a unitary system by a US District Court in 1979.

Wake County's population exploded during the 1980s, increasing from just over 300,000 to more than 425,000 residents. As the newcomers to the county settled outside of Raleigh, concerns rose that an outer ring of more affluent White schools would surround the city. As a solution, WCPSS would need a plan that would bus low-income students of color into suburban schools outside of the city and bus the more affluent White suburban children into schools in the Raleigh central city. Recognizing that community buy-in would be essential, and that simply reassigning students based on their race and/or socioeconomic status was not going to get the degree of buy-in needed, during the 1982–1983 school year, WCPSS developed and instituted a choice plan that included designating 28 schools as magnet schools. Each magnet school was assigned a base neighborhood population, but a significant number of seats were reserved for applicants from across the school district. Students outside of a magnet school's base population applied to enroll in the school, and students were selected to fill available seats by lottery. The plan worked; all 28 magnet schools filled to capacity with both Black and White students (Grant, 2009; McNeal & Oxholm, 2009).

In 1994, in response to less than desirable achievement scores for WCPSS students, Wake superintendent Bill McNeal with the support of the Wake school board set the goal of achieving a 95% test passage rate. WCPSS did not achieve the 95% passage rate goal, but they got pretty close. By 1993, over 91% of WCPSS students in grades 3 through 8 were passing the state reading and math tests. From 1994 to 2003, the test passage rate for economically disadvantaged students went from 55% to 80%. Scores for White and Black students rose, and the gap between the average scores of Black and White students went from 37 points to 17 points. The gap between Hispanic students and White students went from 28 points to 11 points.

Following a 1999 federal court's declaration of unitary status for the nearby Charlotte-Mecklenburg Schools (CMS) and its directive that CMS discontinue the use of race in its student assignment plan, WCPSS decided to revamp its own student assignment policy with the new stated goal of economic integration rather than of racial integration of schools. Under Wake School Policy 6200 adopted in 2000, no WCPSS school was to have more than 40% of its students from low-income families or more than 25% of its students classified as low-achieving (Wake County Public School System, 2000). However, this change in policy did not change the fact that students would be bused across the county, with some students bused for greater distances than others. Up to this point there had not been any serious opposition to the district's student assignment policy, largely because magnet schools did allow for some degree of choice for families, and because schools across the district were considered by most parents to be good schools (Grant, 2009; McNeal & Oxholm, 2009; Silberman, 2002). But a growing number of parents were saying in louder and louder voices that the time had come to end the district's diversity policy and return to neighborhood schools. Parents, particularly more affluent, suburban White parents, but a smaller contingent of economically disadvantaged parents and parents of color as well, were unhappy with (a) not knowing exactly where their children would attend school, (b) not knowing whether their children's assigned school would change from year to year, and (c) having their children bused out of their own neighborhoods to sometimes relatively distant schools. In 2002, a WCPSS parent expressed the growing sentiment of suburban Wake parents in this way: "Diversity by choice is a good thing.... Diversity by forced busing is not" (Richard, 2002).

The 2009 Wake school board election was one of the most contentious elections in the board's history, and even garnered coverage of some national media outlets. New candidates, funded by the John Locke Foundation, a conservative-leaning policy think tank, successfully ran on a platform of ending the district's busing/diversity policies. Each of the board's four contested seats was won by a candidate in favor of ending the district's diversity student assignment policy. These candidates together with one incumbent board member now constituted a majority on the nine-member school board.

It is important to note that WCPSS grew in enrollment from approximately 60 thousand students during the 1990–1991 school year to about 140 thousand students in 2010. Accommodating that explosive growth while still trying to maintain socioeconomically balanced schools across the district resulted in shifting lots of students around the district, and in some limited instances changing students' assignments from one year to the next. While disenchantment had certainly grown with the district's busing students for diversity purposes, in the end, it was likely the combination of busing for diversity purposes and shifting school assignments to accommodate enrollment growth that led to school board turnover in 2009 and the vote to end the busing policy in 2010. Hoxby and Weingarth's (2005) finding that in a single year during that period, only about 16% of WCPSS reassignments were based on solely diversity balancing lends support to this argument. With the most reassignments, they found, factors including but not limited to parent requests, over- and under-crowding of schools, bus routes, and construction all weighed into reassignment decisions.

A series of contentious school board meetings followed the tide-turning 2009 school board election. Unhappy with the direction of the newly elected Wake school board, in February 2010, WCPSS superintendent Del Burns announced his plan to resign effective June 30, 2010. Burns made the following statement in a February 16, 2010 school board meeting:

> Based on personal and obligatory considerations, it is clear to me that I cannot in good conscience continue to serve as superintendent. Therefore, out of respect for the board, out of respect for its directions and its decisions, I provide to the chair written notice that, effective June 30, 2010, I will resign my position.

In an interview following his resignation Burns was quoted as saying: "I will not allow myself to be a pawn in political gamesmanship." In a later interview with a local news reporter Burns added:

> I hold certain values and convictions very, very highly. The proposed policies of the board are not in alignment with my goals and my vision. My person integrity is very important to me.... If I'm going to serve as superintendent, then I have to align with the board. To be effective, a superintendent has to have strong communication with the board, and vice versa. There has to be involvement, and there has to be trust. If I'm not comfortable with the policy direction, then I have to bend or break my principles. That's not something I'm going to do. (Crisson & Burns, 2010)

Burns' public statements regarding the direction of the Wake board drew the ire of the new board majority, which decided in March 2010 to place Burns on administrative leave until his resignation date at the end of June. In the interim, Burns was replaced by Wake chief academic officer Don Hargens Hargens.

Also in March 2010, the newly elected Wake board in a 5–4 vote along party lines, formally made the decision to end the district's long-standing socioeconomic diversity policy that had been heralded nationally for keeping its schools socioeconomically balanced and given the district the reputation of having "no bad schools" (Grant, 2009). A resolution drafted by the board made no mention of diversity, but said that all children can learn at high levels with high-quality instruction. The resolution said also that "the utilization of objective data-driven decisions better supports these efforts than subjective classification and profiling of students." Shortly after the vote to end the busing policy, school board chairman Ronald Margiotta said in a speech to the Northern Wake Republican Club, "We are giving the school system back to the families and taxpayers in this county" (Aarons, 2010, p. 17).

A July 2010 rally hosted by opponents to the district's policy change drew over one thousand supporters. Community and civil rights groups, led by the local chapter of the National Association for the Advancement of Colored People (NAACP), filed a complaint against the Wake board with the US Department of Education's Office for Civil Rights (OCR). OCR responded to the complaint by initiating an investigation into the district's former student assignment policy. In response to an OCR inquiry, WCPSS contended that its former policy had failed to close racial achievement gaps and placed unfair burdens on economically disadvantaged students. The district specifically called attention to the district's graduation rates for Black male students and end-of-grade proficiency rates for economically disadvantaged students, both of which were less than desirable. The board also released data to support its claims (Wake school board to OCR, 2011). As of 2012, OCR investigation was still open.

Also, notably, a collection of groups filed a complaint with AdvancED, the WCPSS's accrediting agency. After a full investigation of the district, AdvancED resolved to place the district on "warned status," and gave them until November 2010 to correct what it deemed to be problems with the district's decision to end the diversity policy. In AdvancED's estimation, the board had ignored student achievement data and acted to advance the personal agendas of board members with its decision to end the socioeconomic diversity policy.

Following the board's decision to end the consideration of socioeconomic status with student assignment, the Wake Education Partnership and the Raleigh Chamber of Commerce partnered with the board to hire a Massachusetts-based education consultant to help develop a new student assignment plan for the district. Based on the consultant's recommendation, the Republican-controlled board decided to move to a *controlled choice* plan. Under controlled choice, all district schools became schools of choice and no students were assigned to a school based solely on their home address. Parents then rank school preferences from a list of schools based on their address. In addition to providing parents with school options, the rationale behind the plan was that parent choices would serve as an indicator of school improvement needs to the district. Board members reasoned that with a choice plan, the presence of under-enrolled schools, particularly in a district such as Wake that is bursting at the seams, would force the district to fix problem schools and keep them competitive for families.

The board voted in December 2010 to hire retired Army Brig. Gen. Anthony Tata as superintendent. Tata school experience included a stint as chief operating office in the DC Public Schools under former chancellor Michelle Rhee. But in September 2012, after only 20 months on the job, the politically embattled Wake school board voted to fire Tata. The board's composition had shifted again during the 2011 elections, and Democrats now held the board majority. The new Democrat majority on the Wake board voted to fire Tata who was hired by the Republican-controlled board 20 months prior, and set their sights on returning to a student assignment policy that considers race among other factors. The four Republican members of the school board charged with Democrat members with voting to fire Tata based on politics. Tata and Democrat members of the board had had a series of public disputes over the district's student assignment plan, and Democrat members charged Tata with being a polarizing figure as the board worked to move past its political division.

The board voted in June 2012, again along party lines, to request that WCPSS staff develop a new student assignment plan that would tie a student's address to specific schools but also attempt to balance schools socioeconomically as well as by student achievement scores. The board's decision to move forward with bringing diversity back into student assignment was not welcome news to all. In addition to the board's Republican minority, the Greater Raleigh Chamber of Commerce did not favor such a move. The Wake Education Partnership also objected to the decision of the Democrat-controlled board. The Wake Education Partnership, a Raleigh-based, local business-supported nonprofit, had opposed ending the socioeconomic diversity policy. But the group had continue to work with the Wake board and a Massachusetts-based education consultant the current *controlled choice* plan.

In December 2012, in a 5–4 vote, the Democrat-controlled board adopted a new student assignment plan for the 2013–2014 school year, ending controlled choice. Under the new plan, students moving into the district will be assigned to a school based on their address. Current WCPSS students will be allowed to remain at the school they currently attend even if the schools is not their assigned school under the new plan. The board will also honor the school selections of current rising sixth and ninth grade students made under the controlled choice plan. The new plan includes limited elements of choice, with parents having a window of time to request a transfer to a school that has available seats. Only 1,500 students will be reassigned under the plan, however, with most reassignments tied to filling seats at a new Wake school.

Final Thoughts

More than a few education scholars, educators, and parents have argued that students benefit from sharing curricular and cocurricular experiences with a diverse set of peers (Chang, Denson, Saenz, & Misa, 2006; Gurin, Nagda, & Lopez, 2004; Whitla et al., 2003). Proponents of racial balance in schools continuing as a top policy priority argue that diversity in schools is so important that individual families should be willing to sacrifice choice and even bear minor inconveniences to achieve racial balance in schools. Choice proponents question how minor those inconveniences are: longer bus rides for children; children attending schools that are great distances away from their homes, making it a challenge for parents to be involved in school activities; and the possibility that children will be reassigned to schools multiple times throughout their academic careers. School diversity advocates argue that having racially balanced schools and diverse school and classroom experiences for children are worth the price of these potential inconveniences. It is very important to note, however, that school diversity advocates are not necessarily opponents of choice, and choice proponents are not necessarily opposed to school diversity; rather it is the case that school diversity proponents believe racial balance should be prioritized over choice, and choice advocates believe choice should be prioritized over racially balancing schools.

The long-term benefits for children of color and White children of attending diverse schools are clear. The United States is a diverse nation that grows more and more colorful and beautiful with each passing year, and American society has benefitted tremendously from *Brown* and the passage of the Civil Rights Act of 1964. Although a great deal of work remains to be done, Black and White Americans have enjoyed getting to know each other in schools, at colleges and universities, as professional colleagues, as neighbors, and through sharing public accommodations. But at what point, if any, should parents' ability to choose a school for their children be limited by societal or school district goals of creating and maintaining racially and socioeconomically balanced schools?

Because so many families of color continue to find their children at the bottom of rankings for student achievement scores and graduation rates, and at the top of lists for suspensions, expulsions, and dropout rates, one might imagine that families of color are playing a prominent role in choice policy conversations across the country; and they are. A tremendous amount of advocacy work has been done in African American and Latino communities. Prominent examples of such efforts include the national work of the Black Alliance for Educational Options (BAEO) and the Hispanic Council for Reform and Educational Options (Hispanic CREO), and the state-level advocacy work of Parents for Educational Freedom in North Carolina (PEFNC). As a result of such organizing and advocacy efforts, parents of color who want greater choice in public education are speaking out. But parents of color have not lined up completely on one side or the other of this debate. While it remains true that Black and Latino children disproportionately attend public schools that have been characterized as failing, generally speaking, it is difficult to gauge Black and Latino parents' feelings about choice policy expansion. Their position is complicated. For many years African Americans, and now Latino communities, have found their political positions on many issues to be in line with the Democratic Party, and as such, communities of color have overwhelmingly supported Democratic candidates in both national and state-level elections. Democratic lawmakers at the national level, and even more important, at the state level, have been aligned with teacher unions for many years; and teacher unions have, generally speaking, opposed the expansion of choice policies. Choice policy nationally has become much less tied to one party or another, as current president Barack Obama, a Democrat, has championed the expansion of charter schools and has funded the expansion of the DC voucher program. But in some states, Democrat legislators wedded to teacher unions continue to fiercely guard against the passage of any choice policies. For example, the absence of a charter school law in Kentucky is tied directly to Democrats' control of the state House of Representatives, and thus, the House Education Committee. Indeed, the existence of choice advocacy organizations that represent people of color such as BAEO and Hispanic

CREO represent both the political divergence of interest groups representing people of color in the United States (DeBray-Pelot et al., 2007), and the emerging divergence of political thought in communities of color. Traditional civil rights groups including the NAACP, the National Urban League, the League of United Latin American Citizens (LULAC), and the Mexican American Legal Defense and Education Fund (MALDEF) have shown either limited or no support for the expansion of choice policies.

That political dynamic has put parents of color who do want additional educational options for their children in a difficult position. Not only are many of their noneducation policy positions in line with the Democratic Party, but over many years, they have grown to trust Democrats, and in many cases, distrust Republicans. These are alliances that have been forged through tough legal and political battles, some of those battles involving these very issues of school desegregation and holding school districts accountable for discriminatory practices. The relationships between Democrats and communities of color, particularly African American communities, are strong; and those relationships have played a significant role in state-level Democratic lawmakers' ability to limit choice policy in some states. Given that reality, there appear to be only a few paths forward for parent choice advocates in states such as Kentucky: advocates can work to change the composition of the state legislature, they can work to weaken the influence that teachers unions have over Democratic legislators, or they can work to convince communities of color to part ways with Democratic lawmakers and teacher unions on choice policy. The mobilization of parents of color has extraordinary potential for pressuring Democrats to support the expansion of choice in the states. While BAEO and Hispanic CREO have engaged in substantial organizing and advocacy work in communities of color already, greater investment in their brand of work could significantly change choice policy outcomes in states where the iron triangle of teacher unions, the traditional public school establishment, and Democratic lawmakers have successfully limited choice policy options.

6

Conclusion

Traditional public school interests in North Carolina, or the BLOB—Big Learning Organizations Bureaucracy—as one study participant referred to them, successfully kept charter schools in a box from the passage of charter school legislation in 1996 until Republicans took control of the state House and Senate in 2011. They did not seek to eliminate charter schools in state. They accepted the state's one hundred–charter school experiment and masterfully played political defense, stopping charter schools from encroaching any further on their territory. While charter schools in North Carolina during that period came to a permanent fixture in the public education landscape, they were a very small one. The majority of North Carolina's one hundred counties did not have any charter schools at all. And even in Wake County, with the state's highest concentration of charter schools, charter school students made up less than 1% of the county's public school enrollment. Charter schools reached their cap in 2001 and after that, the State Board of Education was only able to grant new charters when existing ones were revoked or voluntarily relinquished.

The passage of charter school legislation in North Carolina came at a time when traditional public school interests were most vulnerable. Charter school interests were able to push through passage of charter school legislation during a time that Republicans controlled one chamber of the general assembly. Republican control of the House, however, was very short-lived, resulting in that opportunistic policy window closing rather quickly and making gaining additional ground for charter school interests a near-impossible undertaking.

Traditional public school interests' close relationships with Democrats in the general assembly allowed them to prevent the passage of charter school legislation from being a clean victory for charter school interests. While the advocacy work of groups such as North Carolina Association of Educators (NCAE) and the North Carolina School Boards Association

(NCSBA) was important, of even greater importance was the institutional access these organizations had to Democratic leaders in the general assembly. They enjoyed that access for several reasons. First, NCAE's political action committee donates an extraordinary amount of money to Democratic candidates for political office. Wright (1990), in study of the Congressional Ways and Means Committee found that interest groups' campaign contributions to committee members were an effective way to gain institutional access. The current study's findings support those of Wright. Additionally, a sizeable minority of Democratic general assembly members are vested in traditional public schools, either because they themselves or a close family member spent careers in traditional public schools or because they have very close ties to local school districts. Also, traditional public school employees make up a substantial number of voters. NCAE and the NCSBA contend that these voters vote as a block based on public education issues. While their assertion may or may not be entirely true, many Democratic legislators have grown comfortable with the support in the polls they have enjoyed in the past, and were not likely to gamble with that support to allow for choice policy expansion.

Traditional public school interests have used their institutional access to ensure the blockage of all legislation that would allocate additional funding to charter schools. They adamantly opposed the allocation of any additional funding to charter schools for two reasons. First, local school districts see public school funding as a zero-sum game; funding that goes to charter schools is funding out of the coffers of traditional public school districts. Second, additional funding allocations to charter schools means additional resources for them to be more competitive with traditional public schools.

Charter school advocates in North Carolina celebrated a few minor, but all the same significant, amendments to legislation from 1996–2008. The changes were integral to giving existing charter schools the opportunity to be successful. Charter school operators won a victory with new provisions to the law allowing charter school boards of directors to elect to participate in the state teachers' retirement system. Also significant to the success of charter schools was an early amendment to legislation allowing schools to lease school facilities from sectarian organizations, provided that no religious artifacts are visible. Additionally, a relatively soft interpretation and enforcement of the legislation's racial composition provision was important in keeping the doors of many charter schools open.

Charter school stakeholders and community members formed both formal and informal advocacy organizations. Most of these organizations' work was aimed at raising or removing the charter school cap.

They engaged in the political process through lobbying at the General Assembly, working at the grassroots level to get voters to contact their legislators asking for their support of legislation favorable to charter schools, and working to defeat the local school bonds of school boards that would not pass resolutions in support of lifting the charter school cap. Until 2011, choice policy advocates in North Carolina were unable to build a large enough or powerful enough coalition to have any chance of defeating traditional public school interests and their Democratic allies in the general assembly.

But North Carolina's political landscape changed substantially in 2011. With Republicans taking control of both chambers of the legislature, the outlook for the expansion of choice policies in North Carolina changed immediately. As was the case in 1996 when Republican control of the House of Representatives opened a window for the passage of charter school legislation, Republican takeover in the general assembly in 2011 opened the window of opportunity for choice advocates again. Seizing the opportunity, choice advocates pushed through the passage of legislation to remove the state's charter school cap in 2011. Additionally, after years of grassroots advocacy and applying pressure in the general assembly, North Carolina choice advocates successfully pushed through the passage of a tax credit law for parents of children with special needs. In July 2011, Governor Perdue signed the Tax Credit for Children with Disabilities Act into law, allowing parents of children with disabilities to claim state tax credits for education expenses. The law allows parents up to $6,000 a year in state tax credits for expenses from private school education and therapy for children with special needs.

Choice advocates' window of opportunity opened even wider in 2012 with the election of the state's first Republican governor in over 20 years. Governor McCrory ran for office on an education platform that included expanding educational choices for North Carolina families and students. One area to expect to see policy change could be the passage of a corporate tax credit policy to support private scholarship funding organizations (SFO). Parents for Educational Freedom in North Carolina (PEFNC) has lobbied during previous legislative sessions for a law allowing corporations the option of the diverting their state tax dollars to a SFO. House Bill 1104 introduced in 2012 and sponsored by both Democrat and Republic members, would have allowed the SFO to use donations to distribute scholarships in amounts up to $4,000 per student per year to be used for private school tuition, fees, books, or other school expenses. With the most favorable political landscape North Carolina choice advocates have ever experienced, it is very likely that we will see them push the envelope on choice policy, and do so pretty quickly. They learned the hard lesson after the passage of charter school legislation in 1996 that policy windows can close very quickly.

Implications of Choice Policy Expansion for School Leadership

The passage and expansion of choice policies in the states have significant implications for school leadership practice and leadership preparation. The good and bad news for public school principals is that the trend of decentralizing decision-making authority to the school building level is continuing and even speeding up in states and school districts where parent choice policies are expanding. Choice policies such as charter schools and intra and interdistrict choice policies are forcing the principalship into the mode of executive leadership, assuming more of the roles assumed by independent school headmasters and public school district superintendents (Kowalski & Bjork, 2005) than traditional public school principals.

The executive principal functions as the *decider* for her school. Staffing decisions are ultimately made by the principal who functions as an executive leader. Some readers might be surprised to learn that in many traditional public school districts principals may have little to no input on the hiring of teachers and/or staff members for their school or in making budget decisions. The level of staffing and budgeting decision-making authority principals across the United States enjoy varies considerably. On one end of that continuum, principals in some traditional public school districts show up to school on the first teacher workday of the year, usually in August a few days before students arrive for the first day of school, to meet teachers and staff members for the first time who have been hired by a district administrator over the summer. On the other end of that continuum, some traditional public school principals are responsible for recruiting, interviewing, and making final recommendations for hiring, decisions that must only be approved by the district central office. Although most traditional public school principals exercise staffing authority that rests between those two extremes, it is the rare traditional public school principal who is able to make staffing allocation decisions or hire personnel with only *support* from the district administration. It is much more often the case that district administrators play a more prominent role than the principal in decisions regarding staffing allocations, recruiting, candidate application screening, interviewing, hiring, and even orientation and induction. Choice policies that force decision-making down to the school-level reposition that decision-making authority with the school principal. Further, the repositioning of key decision-making authority to charter school principals is having the effect of forcing traditional public school districts into conversations about the appropriate balance of decision-making authority between school principals and district administrators.

The expansion of choice policies is also requiring that school leaders act more entrepreneurially. This is true not only for principals of charter schools, but for traditional public school principals as well. For generations, traditional public school districts have been able to rely on the district attendance zones to bring students into their doors. The expansion of choice policies, however, provides more parents with school options than ever before. So whether a school is a charter school, a magnet school, or a traditional public school, if families in its locale have school options, schools are put into the position of having to compete to attract and to retain students. Competing to attract and retain students requires that principals begin to think and act more entrepreneurially than public school principals of past generations. In addition to ensuring the school is meeting and ideally exceeding performance standards set by the state, attracting and retaining students requires that principals consider things such as the development of specialty areas, the college acceptance rates and scholarship awards of its graduates, the attractiveness of facilities, the competitiveness of athletic programs, and the variety and viability of cocurricular offerings.

School leadership preparation programs across the United States have by and large prepared aspiring school principals to assume the role of school district middle manager. Because school principals in traditional public schools districts have in most respects functioned as middle managers and not as executives, executive-level leadership preparation has been neither necessary nor practical for aspiring principals. But the expansion of choice policy is forcing leadership preparation programs to consider either revising preparation approaches to accommodate the changing demands of public school leadership in the choice era, or considering alternative tracks for preparing leaders who will assume executive school leadership positions. The Rice Education Entrepreneurship Program (REEP) is one example of a program intended to prepare executive school leaders. Located in Houston, Texas, REEP markets itself as a program that "educates[s] and develop[s] school leaders to run schools as CEOs," with faculty drawn from "among the leading researchers, practitioners and policy makers at the intersection of education and business." Instead of offering the traditional MEd for aspiring school leaders, REEP has degree and program options including an MBA for school leaders, a one-year business training program tailored to educational leaders, and a summer institute for school leaders.

REEP's positioning in the Rice College of Business is not where one would think to look for a school leadership preparation program, but the program and its funders have recognized the changes in the demands of school leadership and have developed an innovative approach intended to prepare aspiring leaders to meet those challenges. Traditional leadership preparation programs in colleges of teacher education will have to reform to meet those demands as well; their continued viability as options for preparing public school leaders depends on it.

Implications of Choice Policy Expansion for Parents and Policy Makers

Parents across the United States have successfully organized and pushed for the passage of legislation to create and expand choice policies in their states and local school districts. The recent removal of the charter school cap and passage of tax credit policy in North Carolina, the passage of expansive education reform policies including provisions for statewide voucher programs in Indiana and Louisiana, the creation and expansion of district choice policies in Charlotte-Mecklenburg (NC) and Wake County (NC), and the creation of the Carter G. Woodson Academy focusing on African American male success in Lexington, KY, are all examples of the expansion of school options for families that have resulted in large part from parents demanding that states and districts (a) provide them with the ability to choose schools for their children and (b) create an array of high-quality school options for parents to choose from. Providing both of these are essential to choice policy having the positive impact on student success that parent choice advocates want.

The passage and expansion of choice policy has undeniably forever changed public education in the United States. Parents like choice and policy makers and educational leaders will now have to find ways to provide it. The days of school districts making school choices for families are coming to an end, admittedly faster in some places than others. But the genie is out of the bottle and there is no going back. Choice has become a central tenet of public education in some states and districts, and is becoming so in others. Even in states where there are no charter school, voucher, or tax credit policies, traditional public school districts are trying to accommodate parents' demand for choice with intradistrict choice policies, attendance zone choice policies, magnet schools, and specialized academies. These districts are finding, however, that it is impossible to accommodate parents' demand for choice without a radical restructuring of their districts. And they will likely come to the realization that even with district restructuring, accommodating demand even within a restructured district is impossible. Policies that open the education market to additional education providers in their locales will be needed.

But real challenges remain even with the passage and expansion of choice policies; challenges that if not tended to, threaten the success of the whole movement. Many of those challenges can be seen clearly in post-Katrina New Orleans. Following the devastation caused by Hurricane Katrina in 2005, the state of Louisiana had both the challenge and opportunity of rebuilding the public school system in New Orleans. It was no secret that the New Orleans public school district prior to Hurricane Katrina had more than its fair share of challenges with student achievement, fiscal responsibility, ethics questions, and even criminal activity. In 2004 approximately two-thirds of the city's public schools were rated *academically unacceptable* under the Louisiana school accountability system, and approximately 67% of the district's students attended a *low-performing school*. Administrative and fiscal incompetence and corruption in the system reached such heights that the FBI set up a satellite office at the district's central office (Horne, 2011).

Now, eight years after Hurricane Katrina, approximately 75% of public schools in the city are charter schools. The vast majority of children in New Orleans attend charter schools. Choice is now central to public education in the city, and things have changed. Most middle-class families prior to Katrina did not consider using the city's public school system, with the exception of a few very elite magnet schools that admitted students based on test scores. Some of these same families now apply for admission to some of the city's high-performing charter schools. State test scores for public school students in New Orleans have risen significantly. It is undeniable that many more children in New Orleans now have the opportunity to attend high-quality public schools. But challenges remain. Jaylee's frustration with finding a high-quality school for her son illustrates some of those challenges.

Jaylee's Story

Jaylee is a young professional mother living in the city of New Orleans. For the last two years, she has worked rather intently to find a school for her son, Jayden, Jr. As most schools in New Orleans are schools of choice, Jaylee has quite a few school options available to choose from; but the process of choosing a school has been much more challenging than she anticipated. While there are many more public school options available to parents such as Jaylee than there were prior to Hurricane Katrina, she and other parents in New Orleans are frustrated by a limited selection of high-quality school options. Jaylee's belief that quality school options are too few in New Orleans has been confirmed by a recent report by the Scott S. Cowen Institute for Public Education Initiatives at Tulane University. The report assesses the success of school choice as a policy of educational reform in New Orleans. The researchers found that the combination of limited seats at high-quality schools and a complicated application process have resulted in a choice system that does an inadequate job of providing all parents in New Orleans quality school choices. Now staring that shortage in the face, as August is approaching and Jayden is preparing to enter Kindergarten, Jaylee has not chosen a school for him. The high-quality schools where she would like to enroll him are of course in high demand. She has applied to these schools, but Jayden has not been selected in any of the school lotteries. With every passing lottery that Jayden's number is not selected, her chances of enrolling him in a high-quality public school in the fall get slimmer.

There are many more high-quality public school options available to Jaylee than there were available to her mother when choosing a school for her. During the 1980s and 1990s, high-quality public school options in New Orleans were extremely limited, and as noted previously, the city's public schools were in far worse condition than they are today. There was only one public elementary school available for Jaylee to attend as a child, and that school along with the majority other schools in the city was a failing one. In 1997, approximately 7% of that school's third and fifth graders passed the state Language Arts or Mathematics examination. Only about 9% of New Orleans Public Schools' third and fifth graders passed the state Language Arts or Mathematics examination. Given the clear shortcomings of both the school and the school district, Jaylee's parents opted out of public schooling for her and sent her to a Catholic school. Her parents' decision was a popular one during that time. Most parents who could afford to do so opted out of public schooling in New Orleans for decades. A plethora of relatively less expensive Catholic school options made opting out of public schooling doable, even for families with modest incomes.

Final Thoughts

So how do policy makers in Louisiana fix the situation that frustrates parents such as Jaylee and seriously jeopardizes the parent choice movement in New Orleans and across the country? Public education traditionalists would argue that choice is responsible for Jaylee's frustration. They are partially correct. Jaylee is frustrated because she has the ability to choose but too few high-quality options available to her. If she did not have the ability to choose, she probably would be less frustrated. More than likely, the district school that Jayden would be assigned to would be a failing one, and Jaylee would either enroll him there or opt out as her parents did and enroll him in a private or parochial school. So yes, it may be her ability to choose that is responsible for her frustration. But taking away a parent's ability to choose would only relieve her frustration with the challenged choice system; taking away a parent's ability to choose does not result in high-quality public schools for all children. Fixing the problem for Jaylee will require policy makers and educational leaders to attend to three policy areas that are key to the success of the parent choice movement: (a) policies that give parents the ability to choose, (b) policies that support the creation of an adequate supply of diverse, high-quality school options for parents, and (c) the enforcement of accountability mechanisms for ensuring that schools of choice meet agreed upon performance standards.

Across the United States, parent choice advocates have exerted a great deal of effort into passing policies that give parents the ability to choose. But for choice policy to realize its potential for success, just as much or more effort and attention must now go into ensuring that once given the ability to choose, there are enough high-quality school options for parents to choose from. Without ensuring that high-quality options are available, parents such as Jaylee have only gained the right to choose from a collection of low-quality schools. Policies must effectively expand the school market to meet parents' demand for schools, and greater efforts must be made to increase the capacity of charter school operators with proven track records of success. Failure to expand the market of high-quality options jeopardizes the success of the entire parent choice movement. Parents and school leaders in New Orleans know very well that there are not enough high-quality schools to go around. The result has been the creation of admissions procedures at some high-performing charter schools with so many preferential criteria that few parents without existing connections to the school or substantial social and political capital have much of a chance to get their children in. Such elaborate preferential admissions processes are unfair and threaten the success of the parent choice movement as well.

Finally, central to ensuring that parents have an ample supply of high-quality school options to choose from, is ensuring that the accountability provisions of choice policies are enforced. Charter school authorizers across the country must consistently hold high standards for granting charters to charter school organizers. The bar for entry into the education market is much too low in some states. Charter authorizers must also consistently hold charters to the agreed upon performance standards spelled out in schools' charters. If a school's charter specifies that it must meet performance standards by a certain date, schools must be held to that standard. Support, especially for new charters, is not sufficient; and policy makers must increase support to help charters meet high standards. But too few persistently low-achieving charter schools across the country continue to operate. Their continued operation jeopardizes the success of the entire parent choice movement, and more importantly, does a disservice to children and families. A competitive education marketplace does allow parents to exercise market accountability by disenrolling their children and taking their public funding elsewhere; but as well, a minimum performance standard must be set for all schools providing educational services for children on the state's behalf.

References

Aarons, D. I. (2010). Bus fight highlights struggles with diversity. *Education Week*. Retrieved from http://www.edweek.org/ew/articles/2010/04/01/28diversity.h29.html

Adamowski, S., Therriault, S. B., & Cavanna, A. P. (2007). *The autonomy gap: Barriers to effective school leadership*. Thomas B. Fordham Foundation & Institute. Retrieved from http://www.edexcellence.net/publications/autonomygap.html

Anderson, L., & Finnigan, K. (2001, April). *Charter school authorizers and charter school accountability*. Paper presented at the Annual Meeting of the American Educational Research Association, Seattle, WA.

Ascher, C., Echazarreta, J., Jacobowitz, R., McBride, Y., Troy, T., & Wamba, N. (2003, March 1). *Charter school accountability in New York: Findings from a three-year study of charter school authorizers*. Charter School Research Project. Retrieved from http://www.eric.ed.gov/ERICDocs/

Associated Press. (1998a, May 4). Charter schools attract Blacks. *The Charlotte Observer*, p. 5C.

Associated Press. (1998b, May 22). Charter schools panel: Drop racial standard. *The Charlotte Observer*, p. 6C.

Austen-Smith, D. (1993). Information and influence: Lobbying for agendas and votes. *American Journal of Political Science, 37*(3), 799–833.

Barr, J., Sadovnik, A., & Visconti, L. (2006). Charter schools and urban education improvement: A comparison of Newark's district and charter schools. *Urban Review, 38*(4), 291–311.

Baumgartner, F. R., & Jones, B. D. (1993). *Agendas and instability in American politics*. Chicago: University of Chicago Press.

Baumgartner, F. R., & Leech, B. L. (1996). The multiple ambiguities of counteractive lobbying. *American Journal of Political Science, 40*(2), 521–542.

Baumgartner, F. R., & Leech, B. L. (2001). Interest niches and policy bandwagons: Patterns of interest group involvement in national politics. *The Journal of Politics, 63*(4), 1191–1213.

Bifulco, R., & Ladd, H. F. (2007). School choice, racial segregation, and test-score gaps: Evidence from North Carolina's charter school program. *Journal of Policy Analysis and Management, 26*(1), 31–56.

Binker, M. (2006, January 19). Charter schools want lottery money. *Greensboro News & Record*, p. B1.

Birkland, T. A. (2005). *An introduction to the policy process: Theories, concepts, and models of public policy making* (2nd ed.). Armonk, NY: M. E. Sharpe.

Blue Ribbon Commission on Charter Schools. (2008). *Report from the Blue Ribbon Commission on charter schools to the North Carolina State Board of Education*. Raleigh: North Carolina State Board of Education.

Bogdan, R. C., & Biklen, S. K. (2003). *Qualitative research for education: An introduction to theories and methods* (4th ed.). Boston: Allyn and Bacon.

Bogdan, R. C., & Biklen, S. K. (2007). *Qualitative research for education: An introduction to theories and methods* (5th ed.). Boston: Allyn and Bacon.

Bonner, L. (2008, October 25). Charter schools divide candidates. *The News & Observer*, p. B1.

Boyd, W. L. (2007). The politics of privatization in American Education. *Educational Policy, 21*(1), 7-14.

Bracey, G. W. (2002). *The war against America's public schools: Privatizing schools, commercializing education*. Boston: Allyn and Bacon.

Brown, F. (1999). North Carolina's charter school law: Flexibility versus accountability. *Education and Urban Society, 31*(4), 465-488.

Buchanan, B. (2002, January 10). State board debates cap on charter schools—The state limit of 100 schools has been reached, and the General Assembly wants a decision made this month. *Greensboro News & Record*, p. B1.

Buchanan, B., & Dyer, E. (2001, January 27). N. C. mulls more charter schools—Some lawmakers want to see a study of whether the state's charter schools are working before deciding to allow more of them. *Greensboro News & Record*, p. A1.

Bulkley, K. (2005). Understanding the charter school concept in legislation: The cases of Arizona, Michigan, and Georgia. *International Journal of Qualitative Studies in Education, 18*(4), 527-554.

Cavanagh, S. (2012, April 18). Louisiana GOP pushes through voucher expansion. *Education Week, 31*(28), 15-17.

Center for Education Reform. (2012). *The essential guide to charter school law: Charter schools laws across the states, 2012*. Retrieved from http://www.edreform.com/wp-content/uploads/2012/04/CER_2012_Charter_Laws.pdf

Chang, M. J., Denson, N., Saenz, V., & Misa, K. (2006). The educational benefits of sustaining cross-racial interaction among undergraduates. *The Journal of Higher Education, 77*(3), 430-455.

Charter school bill faces revamp. (1997, July 25). *The News & Observer*, p. A3.

Charter schools compromise OK'd. (1997, August 12). *The News & Observer*, p. A3.

Charter schools get new faculty rules. (2008, April 4). *The News & Observer*, p. B3.

Charter schools need to meet benchmarks—eventually, the goal is results. (1998, June 28). *Greensboro News & Record*, p. F2.

Charter schools—these are good options but officials must address concerns. (2002, July 23). *The Charlotte Observer*, p. 12A.

Cheng, Y. C. (1996). *School effectiveness and school-based management: A mechanism for development*. Washington, DC: The Falmer Press.

Chubb, J. E., & Moe, T. M. (1988). Politics, markets, and the organization of schools. *The American Political Science Review, 82*(4), 1066-1087.

Chubb, J. E., & Moe, T. M. (1990). *Politics, markets, and American schools.* Washington, DC: Brookings Institution.

Cobb, C. D., Glass, G. V., & Crockett, C. (2000). The U.S. charter school movement and ethnic segregation. Paper presented at the annual meeting of the American Educational Research Association, New Orleans, LA. Retrieved from http://www.leeds.ac.uk/educol/documents/00001410.htm

Cooper, B. S., Fusarelli, L. D., & Randall, E. V. (2004). *Better policies, better schools: Theories and applications.* Boston: Pearson.

Creswell, J. W. (2007). *Qualitative inquiry & research design: Choosing among five approaches.* Thousand Oaks, CA: Sage Publications.

Crisson, S. (Interviewer) & Burns, D. (Interviewee). (2010, March 24). Interview. Retrieved from http://abclocal.go.com/wtvd/story?section=news/local&id=7284486

DeBray-Pelot, E. H., Lubienski, C. A., & Scott, J. T. (2007). The institutional landscape of interest group politics and school choice. *Peabody Journal of Education, 82*(2–3), 204–230.

DiConti, V. D. (1996). *Interest groups and education reform: The latest crusade to restructure the schools.* Lanham, MD: University Press of America.

Douglas, D. M. (1995). *Reading, writing, and race: The desegregation of the Charlotte schools.* Chapel Hill, NC: University of North Carolina Press.

Du Bois, W. E. B. (1935). Does the Negro need separate schools? *Journal of Negro Education, 4*(3), 328–335.

Eberle-Peay, D. (2012). The federal constitution versus a state constitution: Revisiting Zelman v. Simmons-Harris in Indiana. *Journal of Law & Education, 41*(4), 709–721.

Eisenhardt, K. M. (2002). Building theories from case study research. In A. M. Huberman & M. B. Miles (Eds.), *The qualitative researcher's companion* (pp. 5–35). Thousand Oaks, CA: Sage.

Eisner, E. W. (1991). *The enlightened eye: Qualitative inquiry and the enhancement of educational practice.* New York: Macmillan.

Elazar, D. J. (1984). *American federalism: A view from the states.* New York: Thomas Y. Crowell Company.

Epps, K. W. (2007). Charter school loophole urged. *The News & Observer,* p. B5.

Feir, R. E. (1995). *Political and social roots of education reform: A look at the states in the mid-1980s.* Paper presented at the annual meeting of the American Educational Research Association, San Francisco, CA.

Finn, C. E., & Gau, R. L. (1998). New ways of education. *The Public Interest, 130,* 79–82.

Fiske, E. B., & Ladd, H. F. (2000). *When schools compete: A cautionary tale.* Washington, DC: Brookings Institution.

Fowler, F. C. (2004). *Policy studies for educational leaders: An introduction.* Upper Saddle River, NJ: Pearson-Merrill Prentice Hall.

Frank, J., & Bonner, L. (2013). "Coalitions forming across state to be heard at legislature: Left, right prepare for battles in General Assembly." *Charlotteobserver.com.* Retrieved from http://www.charlotteobserver.com/2013/01/29/3821343/coalitions-forming-across-state.html

Frankenberg, E., & Lee, C. (2003). Charter schools and race: A lost opportunity for integrated education. *Education Policy Analysis Archives, 11*(32). Retrieved from http://epaa.asu.edu/ojs/article/download/260/386/

Friedman, M. (1955). The role of government in education. In R. A. Solo (Ed.), *Economics and the public interest* (pp. 123–153). Rutgers, NJ: Rutgers University Press.

Friedman, M. (1997). Public schools: Make them private. *Education Economics, 5*(3), 341–344.

Fuller, H. L. (1985). *The impact of the Milwaukee public school system's desegregation plan on Black students and the Black community (1976–1982).* Unpublished doctoral dissertation. Marquette University, Milwaukee, WI. Retrieved from http://epublications.marquette.edu/dissertations/AAI8526784/

Fuller, H. L. (2000). *The continuing struggle of African Americans for the power to make real educational choices.* Paper presented at the Second Annual Symposium on Educational Options for African Americans, Milwaukee, WI.

Fuller, H. (2002). Educational choice, a core freedom. *The Journal of Negro Education, 71*(1–2), 1–4.

Fuller, B., Gawlik, M., Gonzales, E., & Park, S. (2003). *Charter schools and inequality: National disparities in funding, teacher quality, and student support.* Policy Analysis for California Education, Berkeley, CA.

Fusarelli, L. D. (2001). The political construction of accountability: When rhetoric meets reality. *Education and Urban Society, 33*(2), 157–169.

Fusarelli, L. D. (2002). Texas charter schools and the struggle for equity. In S. Vergari, (Ed.), *The charter school landscape* (pp. 175–191). Pittsburgh, PA: The University of Pittsburgh Press.

Fusarelli, L. D. (2003). *The political dynamics of school choice: Negotiating contested terrain.* New York: Palgrave Macmillan.

Fusareli, L. D. (2008). *Politics of education.* Unpublished manuscript.

Gais, T. L., & Walker, J. L. (1991). Pathways to influence in American politics. In J. L. Walker, Jr. (Ed.), *Mobilizing interest groups in America* (pp. 103–121). Ann Arbor: University of Michigan Press.

Godwin, R. K., Leland, S., Baxter, A., & Southworth, S. (2006). Sinking swann: Public school choice and the re-segregation of Charlotte's public schools. *Review of Policy Research, 23*(5), 983–997.

Goldring, E., & Smrekar, C. (2000). Magnet schools and the pursuit of racial balance. *Education and Urban Society, 33*(1), 17–35.

Goldring, E., & Smrekar, C. (2002). Magnet schools: Reform and race in urban education. *Clearing House, 76*(1), 13–15.

Grant. G. (2009). *Hope and despair in the American city: Why there are no bad schools in Raleigh.* Cambridge, MA: Harvard University Press.

Grbich, C. (2007). *Qualitative data analysis: An introduction.* Thousand Oaks, CA: Sage Publications.

Greene, J. P. (2001). Vouchers in Charlotte. *Education Next, 1*(2), 55–60.

Griffin, A. (1999, January 16). Charter schools' report card on hold, but state gives advice. *The Charlotte Observer,* p. 1C.

Gupta, D. K. (2001). *Analyzing public policy: Concepts, tools, and techniques.* Washington DC: CQ Press.

Gurin, P., Nagda, B. A., & Lopez, G. E. (2004). The benefits of diversity in education for democratic citizenship. *Journal of Social Issues, 60*(1), 17–34.

Gutek, G. L. (2004). *Philosophical and ideological voices in education.* Boston: Pearson.

Hardee, C. (1999, September 5). Charters appear to pass test—the charter school initiative seems to be working despite some financial and accountability problems. *Greensboro News & Record,* p. A1.

Harman, P., Bingham, S. C., & Hood, A. (2002). *An exploratory examination of North Carolina charter schools and their potential impact on white-minority achievement gap reduction.* Paper presented at the annual meeting of the American Educational Research Association, New Orleans, LA.

Hassel, B. C., & Vergari, S. (1999). Charter-granting agencies: The challenges of oversight in a deregulated system. *Education and Urban Society, 31*(4), 406–428.

Heclo, H. (1995). Issue networks and the executive establishment. In D. M. McCool (Ed.), *Public policy theories, models, and concepts* (pp. 262–287). Englewood Cliffs, NJ: Prentice Hall.

Helms, A. D. (2008, February 6). Ruling favors 5 charter schools—They're seeking more money from CMS. *The Charlotte Observer,* p. 2B.

Helms, A. D., & Morrill, J. (2005, May 27). CMS sued over student payments— Charter schools hit set-asides for programs, district calculations. *The Charlotte Observer,* p. 2B.

Hess, F. M. (1999). *Spinning wheels: The politics of urban school reform.* Washington, DC: The Brookings Institute.

Hess, F. M. (2004). The political challenge of charter school regulation. *Phi Delta Kappan, 85*(7), 508–512.

Hirsch, E. (2002). Colorado charter schools: Becoming an enduring feature of the reform landscape. In S. Vergari (Ed.), *The charter school landscape* (pp. 93–112). Pittsburgh, PA: The University of Pittsburgh Press.

Hojnacki, M. (1997). Interest groups' decision to join alliance or work alone. *American Journal of Political Science, 41*(1), 61–87.

Holyoke, T. T. (2003). Choosing battlegrounds: Interest group lobbying across multiple venues. *Political Research Quarterly, 56*(3), 325–336.

Horne, J. (2011). New schools in New Orleans: School reform both exhilarated and imperiled by success. *Education Next, 11*(2), 14–24.

Horsford, S. D. (2010). Mixed feelings about mixed schools: Superintendents on the complex legacy of school desegregation. *Educational Administration Quarterly, 46*(3), 287–321.

Hoxby, C. M. (2003). School choice and school productivity: Could school choice be a tide that lifts all boats? In C. M. Hoxby (Ed.), *The economics of school choice.* Chicago, IL: University of Chicago Press.

Hoxby, C. M., & Weingarth, G. (2005). *Taking race out of the equation: School reassignment and the structure of peer effects.* Working paper. Retrieved from http://www.hks.harvard.edu/inequality/Seminar/Papers/Hoxby06.pdf

Huerta, L. A., & d'Entremont, C. (2007). Education tax credits in a post-Zelman era: Legal, political, and policy alternatives to vouchers. *Educational Policy, 21*(1), 73-109.

Hui, T. K. (2000, September 14). School board feels pressure both ways—Charter schools tied to school bonds. *The News & Observer*, p. A1.

Hula, K. W. (1995). *Lobbying together: Interest group coalitions in legislative politics.* Washington, DC: Georgetown University Press.

John, P. (2003). Is there life after policy streams, advocacy coalitions, and punctuations: Using evolutionary theory to explain policy change? *Policy Studies Journal, 31*(4), 481-498.

John W. Pope Civitas Institute. (2008, January). *January 2008 DecisionMaker Poll.* Retrieved from http://www.jwpcivitasinstitute.org/media/publication-archive/poll-results/january-2008-decisionmaker-poll/

Johnson, D. (2002, January 11). Board recommends raising cap on charters—N. C. ha maximum of 100 schools decision would be legislatures. *The Charlotte Observer*, pp. 4B.

Kafer, K. (2009). A chronology of school choice in the U.S. *Journal of School Choice, 3*(4), 415-416.

Kakadelis, L. (2002, November 13). Cap on charter schools discourages change. *Carolina Journal Online-John Locke Foundation, 629.* Retrieved from www.johnlocke.org/articles/display_story.html?id=382

Kelly, A. P. (2012). Triggering reform at public schools. *Phi Delta Kappan, 93*(6), 46-50.

Kingdon, J. W. (2003). *Agendas, alternatives, and public policies* (2nd ed.). New York: Longman.

Kirst, M. W. (2007). Politics of charter schools: Competing national advocacy coalitions meet local politics. *Peabody Journal of Education, 82*(2-3), 184-203.

Knepper, L. (2006, January 5). Florida Supreme Court strikes down school choice. *Institute for Justice.* Retrieved from http://www.ij.org/florida-school-choice-latest-release

Kolderie, T. (1990). *Beyond choice to new public schools: Withdrawing the exclusive franchise in public education.* Washington, DC: Progressive Policy Institute.

Kowalski, T. J., & Bjork, L. G. (2005). Role expectations of the district superintendent: Implications for deregulating preparation and licensing. *Journal of Thought, 40*(2), 73-96.

Labaree, D. F. (1997). Public goods, private goods: The American struggle over educational goals. *American Educational Research Journal, 34*(1), 39-81.

Lacireno-Paquet, N., & Holyoke, T. T. (2007). Moving forward or sliding backward: The evolution of charter school policies in Michigan and the District of Columbia. *Educational Policy, 21*(1), 185-214.

Liekweg, J. A. (2004). School choice litigation after Zelman and Locke. *Catholic Education: A Journal of Inquiry and Practice, 8*(1), 46-57.

Lee, J. (2004a). Multiple facets of inequity in racial and ethnic achievement gaps. *Peabody Journal of Education, 79*(2), 51-73.

Lee, C. (2004b). *Racial segregation and educational outcomes in metropolitan Boston.* Cambridge, MA: The Civil Rights Project, Harvard University.

Lewis, W. D., & Danzig, A. (2010). Seeing color in school choice. *Journal of School Public Relations, 31*(1), 205–223.

Lewis, W. D., & Fusarelli, W. D. (2010). Leading schools in an era of change: Toward a "new" culture of accountability? In S. D. Horsford (Ed.), *New perspectives on educational leadership: Exploring social, political, and community contexts and meaning* (pp. 111–126). New York, NY: Peter Lang Publishing.

Local Flex, regarding Charter Sch. Teachers Act, NC General Assembly Session Law 2001–462, (2001).

Lubienski, C. (2000). Whither the common good? A critique of home schooling. *Peabody Journal of Education, 75*(1–2), 207–232.

Lubienski, C. (2001). Redefining "public" education: Charter schools, common schools, and the rhetoric of reform. *Teachers College Record, 103*(4), 634–666.

Lubienski, C. (2003). Istrumentalist perspectives on the "public" in public education: Incentives and purposes. *Educational Policy, 17*(4), 478–502.

Lyttle, S. (1998, January 2). Charter school backer talking to 3 firms. *The Charlotte Observer,* p. B5.

Manno, B. V., Finn, C. E., & Vanourek, G. (2000a). Beyond the schoolhouse door: How charter schools are transforming U.S. public education. *Phi Delta Kappan, 81*(10), 736–744.

Mawhinney, H. B. (2001). Theoretical approaches to understanding interest groups. *Educational Policy, 15*(1), 187–214.

Mazzoni, T. L. (1993). The changing politics of state education policy making: A 20-year Minnesota perspective. *Educational Evaluation and Policy Analysis, 15*(4), 357–379.

Mazzoni, T. L., & Malen, B. (1985). Mobilizing constituency pressure to influence state education policy making. *Educational Administration Quarterly, 21*(2), 91–116.

McCarthy, M. (2000). What is the verdict on school vouchers? *Phi Delta Kappan, 81*(5), 371–378.

McLendon, M. K., & Cohen-Vogel, L. (2008). Understanding education policy change in the American states: Lessons from political science. In B. S. Cooper, J. G. Cibulka, & L. D. Fusarelli (Eds.), *Handbook of education politics and policy* (pp. 30–51). New York: Routledge.

McNeal, L. R. (2009). The re-segregation of public education now and after the end of *Brown v. Board of Education. Education and Urban Society, 41*(5), 562–574.

McNeal, B., & Oxholm, T. (2009). *A school district's journey to excellence: Lessons from business and education.* Thousand Oaks, CA: Corwin Press.

McNiff, M. G., & Hassel, B.C. (2002). Charter schools in North Carolina: Confronting the challenges of rapid growth. In S. Vergari (Ed.), *The charter school landscape* (pp. 208–229). Pittsburgh, PA: University of Pittsburgh Press.

Meredith v. Jefferson County School Board, 126 S.Ct. 2351 (2006).

Merriam, S. B. (1998). *Qualitative research and case study applications in education*. San Francisco: Jossey-Bass.

Merriam, S. B. (2002). *Qualitative research in practice: Examples for discussion and analysis*. San Francisco: Jossey-Bass.

Mickelson, R. A. (2001). Subverting Swann: First- and second-genderation segregation in Charlotte, North Carolina. *American Educational Resources Journal, 38*(2), 215–252.

Mickelson, R. A., & Ray, C. A. (1994). Fear of falling from grace: The middle class, downward mobility, and school desegregation. *Research in Sociology of Education and Socialization, 10,* 207–238.

Mickelson, R. A., & Southworth, S. (2005). When opting out is not a choice: Implications for NCLB's transfer option from Charlotte, North Carolina. *Equity & Excellence, 38*(3), 249–263.

Minchin, M. (2011, July 17). "Family's crusade leads to new law." *Charlotteobserver.com*. Retrieved from http://www.charlotteobserver.com/2011/07/17/2454826/familys-crusade-leads-to-new-law.html

Mintrom, M. (2002). Michigan's charter school movement: The politics of policy design. In S. Vergari (Ed.), *The charter school landscape* (pp. 74–92). Pittsburgh, PA: University of Pittsburgh Press.

Miron, G. J. (2008). The shifting notion of "publicness" in public education. In B. S. Cooper, J. G. Cibulka, & L. D. Fusarelli (Eds.), *Handbook of education politics and policy* (pp. 338–349). New York, NY: Routledge.

Mitchell, G. A. (1989). *An evaluation of state-financed school integration in metropolitan Milwaukee*. Wisconsin Policy Research Institute.

Munn, L. H. (2001, February 4). Should the state remove the cap on the number of charter schools? *The Charlotte Observer*, p. 2U.

Murphy, J., & Shiffman, C. D. (2002). *Understanding and assessing the charter school movement*. New York: Teachers College Press.

Nathan, J. (1996). *Charter schools: Creating hope and opportunity for American education*. San Francisco: Jossey-Bass.

Nathan, J. (2002). Minnesota and the charter public school idea. In S. Vergari (Ed.), *The charter school landscape* (pp. 17–31). Pittsburgh, PA: University of Pittsburgh Press.

National Alliance for Public Charter Schools. (2008). "Caps on charter schools." Retrieved from http://www.publiccharters.org/section/issues/stateleg/caps/

New campaign touts charter schools. (2006, November 3). *The News & Observer*, p. B3.

Ni, Y., & Arsen, D. (2011). School choice participation rates: Which district are pressured? *Education Policy Analysis Archives, 19*(29), 1–26.

Olson, M. (1965). *The logic of collective action: Public goods and the theory of groups*. Cambridge, MA: Harvard University Press.

Opfer, D. V. (2001). Beyond self-interest: Educational interest groups and congressional influence. *Educational Policy, 15*(1), 135–152.

Opfer. D. V., Young, T. V., & Fusarelli, L. D. (2008). Politics of interest: Interest groups and advocacy coalitions in American education. In B. S. Cooper, J. G.

Cibulka, & L. D. Fusarelli (Eds.), *Handbook of education politics and policy* (pp. 195-216). New York, NY: Routledge.

Orfield, G., & Lee, C. (2007). *Historic reversals, accelerating resegregation, and the need for new integration strategies*. Los Angeles, CA: Civil Rights Project at UCLA.

Orr-Bement, D. M. (2002). *A theoretical perspective of the state policy process for higher education policy decisions*. Paper presented at the annual meeting of the Association for the Study of Higher Education, Sacramento, CA.

Parents Involved in Community Schools (PICS) v. Seattle School District No. 1, 127 S.Ct. 2738 (2007).

Peterson, P. E., & Hassel, B. C. (1998). *Learning from school choice*. Washington, DC: Brookings Institution.

Portz, J. (1996). Problem definitions and policy agendas: Shaping the educational agenda in Boston. *Policy Studies Journal, 24*(3), 371-386.

Price, J. (1998, April 29). Charter schools feel money pinch. *The News & Observer*, p. A1.

Public Schools First NC. (2012). *Website*. Retrieved from http://www.public-schoolsfirstnc.org/

Rawlins, W. (1997a, June 25). Charter school changes sought. *The News & Observer*, p. A1.

Rawlins, W. (1997b, July 3). Charter bill advances. *The News & Observer*, p. A3.

Renzulli, L. A., & Roscigno, V. J. (2005). Charter school policy, implementation, and diffusion across the United States. *Sociology of Education, 78*(4), 344-365.

Report: Keep charter school cap. (2007, June 7). *The News & Observer*, p. B1.

Richard, A. (2002). Broad effort to mix student by wealth under fire in N.C. *Education Week, 21*(37), 1.

Robelen, E. W. (2006, August 22). NAEP reanalysis finds lag in charter school scores. *Education Week, 26*(1). Retrieved from http://www.edweek.org/ew/articles/2006/

Robelen, E. W., & Cavanagh, S. (2008). Voucher, evolution in La. *Education Week, 27*(43), 17-20.

Robinson, S. E. (2004). Punctuated equilibrium, bureaucratization, and budgetary changes in schools. *Policy Studies Journal, 32*(1), 25-39.

Rochefort, D. A., & Cobb, R. W. (1994). Problem definition: An emerging perspective. In D. A. Rochefort & R. W. Cobb (Eds.), *The politics of problem definition: Shaping the policy agenda* (pp. 1-31). Lawrence: University Press of Kansas.

Rumberger, R. W., & Palardy, G. J. (2002). *The impact of student composition on academic achievement in Southern high schools*. Los Angeles, CA: The Civil Rights Project, UCLA. Retrieved from http://civilrightsproject.ucla.edu/

Sabatier, P. A., & Jenkins-Smith, H. (1999). The advocacy coalition framework. In P. Sabatier (Ed.), *Theories of the policy process* (pp. 117-166). Boulder, CO: Westview Press.

Salisbury, R. H. (1990). The paradox of interest groups in Washington: More groups, less clout. In A. King (Ed.), *The new American political system* (2nd ed.) (pp. 203-229). Washington DC: AEI Press.

Sass, T. R. (2006). Charter schools and student achievement in Florida. *Education Finance and Policy, 1*(1), 91–122.

Schnattschneider, E. E. (1960). *The semi-sovereign people.* New York: Holt, Rinehart, and Winston.

Scientific Software Development. (2004). *ATLAS.TI: The knowledge workbench Version WIN 5.0.* Berlin: Scientific Software Development.

Scott, J., Lubienski, C., & DeBray-Pelot, E. (2009). The politics of advocacy in education. *Educational Policy, 23*(1), 3–14.

Shober, A. F., Manna, P., & Witte, J. F. (2006). Flexibility meets accountability: State charter school laws and their influence on the formation of charter schools in the United States. *Policy Studies Journal, 34*(4), 563–587.

Silberman, T. (1999, November 25). Cap on charter schools is near. *The News & Observer*, p. B1.

Silberman, T. (2002). Wake County schools: A question of balance. In R. Kahlenberg (Ed.), *Divided we fail* (pp. 141–166). New York, NY: Century Foundation.

Simmons, T. (1999, July 21). State tests trip charter school. *The News & Observer*, p. B1

Sims, C. H., & Miskel, C. G. (2003). The punctuated equilibrium of national reading policy: Literacy's changing images and venues. In W. Hoy & C. G. Miskel (Eds.), *Studies in leading and organizing schools* (pp. 1–26). Greenwich, CT: Information Age.

Spitzer, R. J., Ginsberg, B., Lowi, T. J., & Weir, M. (2002). *Essentials of American politics.* New York: W. W. Norton & Company.

Spring, J. (2005a). *Conflict of interests: The politics of American education.* Boston: McGraw Hill.

Spring, J. (2005b). *Political agendas for education: From the religious right to the Green Party.* Mahwah, NJ: Lawrence Erlbaum Associates.

Stewart, T., Wolf, P. J., & Cornman, S. Q. (2005). *Parent and student voices on the first year of the DC Opportunity Scholarship Program* (Report No. SCDP 05–01 SUM). School Choice Demonstration Project, Georgetown University, Washington, DC. Retrieved from http://www.aecf.org/

Stewart, T., Wolf, P. J., & Cornman, S. Q. (2007). Parent and student voices on the first year of the DC opportunity scholarship program. *Peabody Journal of Education, 82*(2–3), 311–386.

Stoddard, C., & Corcoran, S. P. (2006). The political economy of school choice: Support for charter schools across states and school districts. *Journal of Urban Economics, 62*, 27–54.

Stone, D. A. (2002). *The art of political decision making* (revised ed.). New York: W. W. Norton.

Stoops, T. (2007, May). *Ten years of excellence: Why charter schools are good for North Carolina.* Raleigh, NC: John Locke Foundation.

Stulberg, L. M. (2007, June). *Beyond the battle lines: Lessons from New York's charter caps fight.* Seattle, WA: National Charter School Research Project. Retrieved from http://www.crpe.org/cs/crpe/download/csr_files/pub_ncsrp_battlelines_jun07.pdf/

Thompson, E. (1998, March 5). Charter schools not meeting racial rules. *The Charlotte Observer*, p. 3C.

True, J. L., Jones, B. D., & Baumgartner, F. R. (1999). Punctuated-equilibrium theory: Explaining stability and change in American policymaking. In P. Sabatier (Ed.), *Theories of the policy process* (pp. 97–115). Boulder, CO: Westview Press.

Vaden, T. (2002, August 11). It's too soon to expand charter schools in North Carolina. *The Chapel Hill News*, p. A5.

Van Horn, C. E., Baumer, D. C., & Gormley Jr., W. T. (1989). *Politics and public policy*. Washington, DC: CQ Press.

Vergari, S. (2007). The politics of charter schools. *Educational Policy, 21*(1), 15–39.

Wake County Public School System. (2000). *Wake County Policy 6200, Student Assignment*. Raleigh, NC: Author.

Wake school board to OCR: Diversity policy was unfair. (2011, April 3). *WRAL News*. Retrieved from http://www.wral.com/news/education/wake_county_schools/story/9378475/

Walch, T. (1984). Tuition tax credits: Historical and hopeful perspective. *Momentum, 15*(1), 20–23.

Washington shoots down charter school loan plan. (1997, April 4). *Greensboro News & Record*, p. B2.

Weisenberger, A. (2001). Cleveland program could lead to definitive Supreme Court precedent on school vouchers. *Journal of Law & Education, 30*(3), 564–570.

Welner, K. G. (2008). *Neo vouchers: Providing public funds for private schools through tuition tax credits*. Lanham, MD: Rowman & Littlefield.

Whitla, D. K., Orfield, G., Silen, W., Teperow, C., Howard, C., Reede, J. (2003). Educational benefits of diversity in medical school: A survey of students. *Academic Medicine, 78*(5), 460–466.

Winters, M. A., & Greene, J. P. (2011). Public school response to special education vouchers: The impact of Florida's McKay scholarship program on disability diagnosis and student achievement in public schools. *Educational Evaluation and Policy, 33*(2), 138–158.

Witte J. F., Sterr, T. D., Thorn, C. A. (1995, December). *Fifth year report: Milwaukee parental choice program*. Department of Political Science and Robert M. La Follette Institute of Public Affairs, University of Wisconsin, Madison. Retrieved from http://www.lafollette.wisc.edu/publications/workingpapers/MilwaukeeChoice5YR/fifthYear.html

Wolf, P. J., Peterson, P. E., & West, M. R. (2001, August). *Results of a school voucher experiment: The case of Washington, DC after two years*. Paper presented at the Annual Meeting of the American Political Science Association, Washington, DC. Retrieved from http://papers.ssrn.com/sol3/papers.cfm?abstract_id=313822

Wong, K. W., & Shen, F. X. (2002). Politics of state-led reform in education: Market competition and electoral dynamics. *Educational Policy, 16*(1), 161–192.

Wong, K. K., & Langevin, W. E. (2007). Policy expansion of school choice in the American states. *Peabody Journal of Education, 82*(2–3), 440–472.

Wright, J. R. (1990). Contributions, lobbying, and committee voting in the U.S. House of Representatives. *American Political Science Review, 84*(2), 417–438.

Yin, R. K. (2003). *Case study research: Design and methods* (3rd ed.). Thousand Oaks, CA: Sage Publications.

Young, T. V., Lewis, W. D., Tate, N., Grant, C. P., & Thomas, S. (2008). *The art of agenda setting: Governors' use of problem definition in state of the state addresses*. Paper presented at the annual meeting of the American Political Science Association, Boston, MA.

Ziebarth, T. (2007). Issue brief: Peeling the lid off state-imposed charter school caps. *National Alliance for Public Charter Schools*. Retrieved from http://www.uscharterschools.org/cs/sp/lpt/uscs_rs/2276/

Zimmer, R., & Buddin, R. (2007). Getting inside the black box: Examining how the operation of charter schools affects performance. *Peabody Journal of Education, 8*(2–3), 231–273.

Index

accountability
    charter schools, 43–4, 73, 75, 76, 80–1, 98–101
    teachers, 87–8
African Americans, 17, 25–6, 62, 139–41
    African American students, 2–3, 17–18, 25, 31, 66, 123, 139–41
American Education Reform Council, 18
American Federation of Teachers, 41, 48, 53
Americans United for Separation of Church and State, 35
Annie E. Casey Foundation, 17
Arizona, 16, 35, 42, 65–7, 125
    Arizona Education Association, 35
    Arizona School Boards Association, 35

Black Alliance for Educational Options (BAEO), 12, 17, 39, 140
Blaine Amendment (defined), 34
Boehner (Rep. John), 30
Bradley Foundation, 18
Budde, Ray, 41
Bush (President George W.), 29, 39
busing, 25, 131–9

California, 37
    Compton Unified School District, 37
    Parent Revolution, 37
Center for Education Reform, 39, 70
Charter schools (defined), 15, 16, 19–20
    admissions, 74, 108–9

authorizers, 66, 71, 98
autonomy, 42–3
boards, 71, 73, 77, 81, 85
caps, 92, 93–7
facilities, 77, 81, 101–7
funding, 71, 78, 81, 87, 101–7
oversight, 71, 97–101
policy adoption, 61–3
policy waivers, 88–9
teachers, 74, 78, 82, 85, 87–8, 109–13
Charter Schools Expansion Act, 41
Children's Scholarship Fund, 23, 24
Choice Incentive Fund, 39
Clinton (President Bill), 41
Colorado, 68–9

Daniel Foundation, 18
District of Columbia (DC)
    charter schools, 71
    Opportunity Scholarship Program, 29
    Washington Scholarship Fund, 24–5, 29
desegregation (and segregation), 20–1, 25, 89, 123–40
Du Bois, W.E.B., 123

Educational CHOICE Charitable Trust, 23
educational leadership, 146–8
    leadership preparation, 147–8
Educational Opportunities Act, 39
Establishment Clause (US Constitution), 15, 26, 28, 35

Florida
  McKay Scholarship Program, 16, 31–2
  Opportunity Scholarships
    Program, 16, 31
Fordham Foundation, 17
Friedman Foundation for Educational
  Choice (Milton & Rose Friedman
  Foundation), 18
Friedman, Milton, 23–4
Fuller, Howard, 17
Fund for Innovation in Education, 39

Gates (Bill & Melinda) Foundation, 17
Georgia, 65–7
Greater Educational Opportunities
  Foundation, 39

Hispanic Council for Reform and
  Educational Options (CREO), 18,
  39, 140
Hispanic students, 18, 27, 31, 62, 123

llinois, 36
  Illinois Federation of Teachers, 36
Improving America's Schools Act, 41
interdistrict choice policy, 15, 21–3
intradistrict choice policy, 21–2
Indiana
  Choice Scholarship Program, 32
Iowa, 15

Kentucky, 88–9
  Carter G. Woodson Academy, 2–3
  Fayette County Public Schools
    (FCPS), 2–3
  Jefferson County Public Schools
    (Louisville), 22
  Jefferson County Teachers'
    Association, 53
  Kentucky Charter Schools
    Association, 12
  Kentucky Education Association
    (KEA), 53

Louisiana
  Jindal, Governor Bobby, 33–4
  Louisiana Federation of Teachers,
    33–4
  New Orleans, 33–4, 149–51
  New Orleans Public Schools, 11
  St. Charles Parish Public Schools, 12
  Student Scholarships for
    Educational Excellence
    Program, 33
  United Teachers of New Orleans
    (UTNO), 12
low-income students, 15, 17–18, 22–3,
  26–7, 28, 29, 32, 33, 35, 129–39

Magnet schools, 20–1
  Magnet Schools Assistance
    Program, 20–1
Michigan, 22, 65
  Michigan Education Association, 65
  Schools of Choice Program, 22
Minnesota, 15, 41, 50, 54
Mississippi, 42
  charter schools, 82–5
Mueller v. Allen, 15

National Association of Elementary
  School Principals, 48, 49
National Alliance for Public Charter
  Schools, 16
National Education Association
  (NEA), 48, 50–2, 53, 64–5
National School Boards Association,
  48, 51–2
New York, 67–8
  United Federation of Teachers
    (UFT), 64–5
No Child Left Behind (NCLB), 38–9
North Carolina
  Allison, Darrell, 121–2
  Allred, (Rep. Cary), 95, 112
  Americans for Prosperity North
    Carolina, 114
  Asheville City School District, 104
  Blackwood, (NC Rep. Curtis), 96
  Blue Ribbon Commission on
    Charter Schools, 96–7
  Bourger, (NC Sen. Doug), 96

INDEX 167

Charlotte, 24, 131
Charlotte-Mecklenburg Schools, 104–5, 131–3
charter schools, 74–8, 91–122
Charter School Advisory Committee, 94, 95, 97–8, 99, 128, 129
Capacchione v. Charlotte-Mecklenburg
Coble, Ran, 96
Daughtry, (NC Rep. Leo), 94, 112
Devitt, Wayne, 95
Francine Delaney School, 104
Garrou, (NC Sen. Linda), 96
Gerber, Roger, 93
Goodall, (NC Sen. Eddie), 96
Gulley, (NC Sen. Wib), 95, 106, 108, 112
Hensley, (NC Rep. Bob), 109
Humble, Tom, 97
Imagine Schools, 114
John Locke Foundation, 92, 97, 113
John W. Pope Civitas Institute, 92
Killian, (NC Rep. Ric), 96
Kirk, Phil, 94
League of Charter Schools (NC), 93, 114
Lewis, (NC Rep. David), 96
Lundy, Bob, 97
McCrory, (NC Governor Pat), 118–19, 121–2, 145–6
Morey, Liz, 93–4
Moyer, Jack, 97
North Carolina Association of Educators (NCAE), 12, 53–4, 108, 116, 118–19, 143–4
North Carolina Association of School Administrators, 117–18
North Carolina Center for Public Policy Research (NCPPR), 95, 96
North Carolina Education Alliance, 113
North Carolina Education Lottery, 107
North Carolina School Boards Association, 108, 114–15, 117–18, 143–4

North Carolina State University, 12
Office of Charter Schools (Department of Public Instruction), 97
Parents for Educational Freedom in North Carolina (PEFNC), 18–19, 113, 121, 145
Perdue (NC Governor Bev), 52–3, 119, 120
Public Schools First NC, 122
Raleigh, 133
Shaw, (NC Sen. Larry), 96
Shubert, (NC Rep. Fern), 102
Smith, (NC Sen. Fred), 96
Stoops, Terry, 97
Swan v. Charlotte-Mecklenburg Board of Education, 131
Vinroot, Richard, 104
Wake Education Partnership, 138
Wake County Public School System (WCPSS), 12, 133–9
Wood (NC Sen. Steve), 91
Ziko (Attorney General Thomas), 104, 105

Ohio
  charter schools, 71–4
  Cleveland City Schools, 27
  Ohio Federation of Teachers, 28
  Pilot Project Scholarship Program, 27
Obama (President Barack), 30

Paige (US Education Secretary Rod), 39
Parent Trigger Laws, 36–8
Parents Involved in Community Schools (PICS) v. Seattle School District No. 1, 129–30
Pennsylvania, 36
People for the American Way, 35
Pisces Foundation, 17
politics
  going public, 54
  grass-roots advocacy, 113–14
  incrementalism, 44
  interest groups, 47–58; coalitions, 49
  litigation (strategy), 54

politics—*Continued*
  lobbying (strategy), 52–8, 113–14
  pluralism, 48
  policy monopolies, 44–7
  political action committees (PACs) (strategy), 52–3
  political culture, 65
  problem definition (strategy), 61–5, 65–6; focusing events, 61
  punctuated equilibrium, 44–7
  rational choice, 50–2
  venue shopping (strategy), 56–8
public education (defined), 4, 7
public goods and private goods, 6–7, 52
public schooling, 4–5

qualitative research
  archival documents, 9–10, 11
  conformability, 10
  credibility, 10
  data analysis, 9–10
  field notes, 8–9
  interviews, 8–9
  realism (epistemology), 12–13
  subjectivity (author's), 11

Race to the Top, 93
Rubio (US Senator Marco), 39

Scholarships for Opportunities and Results (SOAR) Act, 20

school vouchers (private), 16, 23, 24
school vouchers (public), 15, 16, 23–34
Shanker, Albert, 41
special education, 16, 31–2
student assignment, 22, 129–30, 131–40

tax credits policy, 15, 16, 34–6, 39
  scholarship granting organizations (SGOs), 35, 39
  Tax Payer Relief Act of 1997, 34
teachers unions, 26, 28, 33, 35, 36, 41, 48, 50–2, 53–4, 64–5, 67, 68, 69, 108, 116, 118–19, 143–4
Texas, 68–9
Thompson, Tommy, 26

US Conference of Mayors, 37

Walton Family Foundation, 17
Wisconsin
  Institute for the Transformation of Learning (Marquette University), 17
  Milwaukee Parental Choice Program, 26
  Milwaukee Public Schools, 25–7
  Williams, (WI Rep. Polly), 26
Wyoming
  charter schools, 78–82

Zelman v. Simmons-Harris, 28–9

GPSR Compliance
The European Union's (EU) General Product Safety Regulation (GPSR) is a set of rules that requires consumer products to be safe and our obligations to ensure this.

If you have any concerns about our products, you can contact us on

ProductSafety@springernature.com

In case Publisher is established outside the EU, the EU authorized representative is:

Springer Nature Customer Service Center GmbH
Europaplatz 3
69115 Heidelberg, Germany

www.ingramcontent.com/pod-product-compliance
Lightning Source LLC
LaVergne TN
LVHW021717060526
838200LV00050B/2705